PRAISE FOR

THE BLUNDER YEARS

"Like David Sedaris, it's the way Caragol tells his stories that make them so damn funny. Each chapter is a tiny time machine that transports you someplace unexpected."

— BRUCE LEWIS, AUTHOR OF THE *ANGEL OF MERCY* SERIES

"*The Blunder Years* features the best elements of storytelling. Phil Caragol shows great affection for the characters in the often hilarious tales that make up this book. His observations are wise, irreverent, and at times, quite poignant. It's a terrific read!"

— PETER CAMMANN, AUTHOR OF *THE FLIES ARE TOO DAMN SMALL: ADVENTURES OF A DEEPLY FLAWED ANGLER* AND *FISHING VERMONT'S LAKES & STREAMS*

"Caragol brings a fresh voice to oral history with *The Blunder Years*—an entertaining, thoughtful, and reflective rite of passage through the baby boom era."

— JOHN HUMBOLDT GATES, AUTHOR OF *NIGHT CROSSINGS*

"Witty, heartfelt, a vivid snapshot of childhood mischief and teenage rebellion."

— NICK PIROG, BEST-SELLING AUTHOR OF THE *THOMAS PRESCOTT* AND *3:00 AM SERIES*

Cover Photo: Me with my big brother, Richie, Christmas 1957 in the lawless Long Island territory, hellbent on dispensing justice with the blazing fury of six-shooter cap guns.

Visit **www.PhilCaragol.com** for more vintage photos of the family, friends, and lunatics in these 95% true stories.

THE BLUNDER YEARS

A Boyhood Memoir

PHIL CARAGOL

Rocketship
Books

Fourth-grade class photo at Our Lady of Victory, Long Island. Me: Top row second from right. Stevie McCarthy: Second row from top, far left, smited for impure thoughts by the blinding light of the Almighty.

ISBN: Paperback 979-8-9921020-0-0; Hardcover 979-8-9921020-1-7

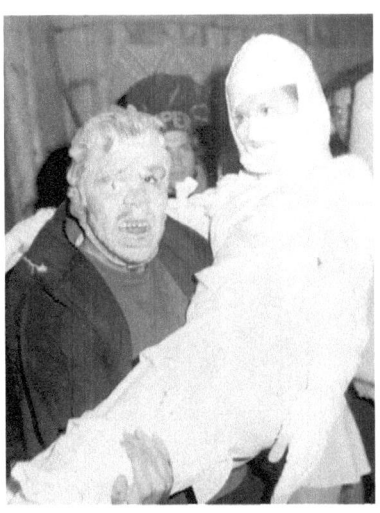

For Susie, my love, friend, professional editor, cheerleader, therapist, and corrections officer since 1974.

CONTENTS

INTRODUCTION

"They say good stories are never written by mistake and that mistakes make good stories. I have no idea who 'they' are, but I think they're onto something."
- Phil C.

The summer after my father's funeral, I flew from San Francisco to visit my lonely, discombobulated mom on her seventy-third birthday. I overheard her in the kitchen opening and closing cupboard doors, rustling through piles of bills on the breakfast table, and grumbling to herself in her Brooklyn accent. "Come on, ya can find it. Ya know *way-ah* it is. Ya know *what* it is. Ya came in he-ah for a reason, d'intcha? Think, Dorothy! Think!"

I realized then that Mom's short-term memory wasn't as sharp as it used to be, even with the assistance of her pep talk to herself. But if I asked her about something that happened 60 years ago, she announced the answer like a Nobel Prize-winning historian with a rapid-fire encyclopedic memory.

"Mom, what was the name of that Hatt girl in your fifth-grade class in 1929?"

"Ya mean, Iona? Iona Hatt? She awlso had two olda sistas, Ura and Ima, and a younga brutha, Richard, but everybody cawled him Dick." I waited for the punchline I'd heard a hundred times before. "Those kids grew up tough. My hat's awff to them."

While Iona, Ura, Ima, and Dick Hatt's names sounded like a page from a book of unfortunate urban legends, an old classmate of Mom's confirmed that those were indeed the actual names bestowed on the Hatt kids by their apparently unstable and sadistic parents. Mom had remembered and rattled off the name of every Hatt as if she had just seen them fling their Depression-era cloche, beret, and fedora chapeaus skyward in a schoolyard hooray of Mad Hatterness.

That brings me to why I wrote this boyhood memoir, *The Blunder Years*, at age 71.

There are fleeting moments when I, too, now walk into the kitchen, office, or garage with an irritating imaginary question mark floating above my head.

Like a blinking yellow caution light at the intersection of my short- and long-term memories, I wonder if the question mark is merely asking, *Tell me again— why are you in this room, and what are you looking for?* Or is it asking deeper questions about the slipping state of my recall abilities? *Are you losing your marbles? Did your elevator peter out on the 71st floor and start its descent to the underground nursing home? Are you becoming a human replica of M.T., the forgetful patriarch of the Hatt family?*

I wrote *The Blunder Years* as a long-term memory test and a first-hand account of what it was like to grow up on Long Island in the 1950s, '60s, and '70s as a baby boom kid. I was raised by Catholic parents who were the religious equivalents of the Pope and Mother Theresa in a town where Catholics outnumbered trees by two-to-one, and my Catholic melting pot of friends had names like Joey Scalisi, Tommy McInerney, and Pawlina Pakenowsky.

These stories are true as I recollect them and recount the blunders I made in my youth, due in part to a full-blown case of ADHD, an undiagnosed condition back in the day.

All I wanted to be was a normal kid instead of a human ping-pong ball with the impulse control and attention span of an over-caffeinated squirrel.

My kindergarten teacher, Mrs. Goldberg, figured out my problem and broke the bad news to my parents. "Mr. and Mrs. Caragol, I'm sorry to report—based on years of kindergarten experience—that your son is severely scatterbrained." Of course, my mom and dad already knew that. It's pretty obvious when you're raising a ping-pong ball.

If you doubt these stories are true, I can't blame you. Even close friends have cocked their heads like befuddled Labrador Retriever puppies when they hear my stories and question them in polite silence...

No way your Maypole dance in kindergarten sent mothers running out of the room. I don't buy it.

How could you possibly convince an entire Boy Scout patrol that Russia AND China just launched nuclear missiles at New York, and you were all toast?

How weird would you have to be to eat a lawn bag of communion wafers? Who does that?

Seriously, who disguises himself as a little cat burglar and prowls the neighborhood kidnapping garden gnomes?

I hope these boyhood stories give my fellow boomers a lighthearted and heartwarming blast from our shared past and give younger readers a taste of what it was like to come of age in the Blunder Years.

I'm immensely grateful to each of you, not only for reading this book, but for reading this far.

I wish I had your attention span.

❧ I ❧
THE RUG RAT YEARS
1953-1965 A.D.H.D.

Young me and Richie demonstrating 1958 car-safety
Worst Practices.

MR. CLEAN AND THE OCTOPUS

"Tranquilizers work only if you follow the advice on the bottle—
keep away from children."
- Phyllis Diller

O n May 3, 1953, a masked anesthesiologist knocked my mother out cold while my father told lawyer jokes, played cards, and smoked Cuban cigars down the hall in the husband's waiting room. Long Island's Mercy Hospital operated at full baby-boom capacity, a fine-tuned delivery machine that cranked out more new models per day than Ford produced cars in a year. Efficient output ruled out slow-acting sedatives, interfering husbands, and time-consuming C-sections—a term more commonly used to describe the worst seating area behind a pillar at a Broadway musical.

I rolled off the line into a post-war world and booby-trapped home where my parents never used the words "child" and "safety" in the same sentence.

For starters, my sweet mother left me alone on the front lawn in a baby carriage on sweltering summer afternoons for doctor-recommended fresh-air naps. I was a helpless newborn lawn gnome parked on a postage-stamp yard on a bustling street. Luckily, I evaded abduction by kidnappers and attacks by birds of prey, stray dogs, and the sole aggressive squirrel that roamed our neighborhood. My missing-baby picture never appeared on milk cartons, an impossibility anyway because milk only came in glass bottles with limited advertising space.

Cars had no seatbelts until 1968. On the positive side, I had an unobstructed front-seat view on my mother Dot's lap, my face within burping distance of the windshield, as my father Lou careened down the highway. On the negative side, if my lead-footed pop plowed us into an oncoming car, Mom and I would have flown through the glass while gawkers watched the woman clutching a baby soar across the highway like a missile in a red and white polka dot dress.

In my toddler years, I felt privileged to bounce around in the back seat with my older sister and brothers. With no child seat or automatic window and door locks in our wood-paneled DeSoto station wagon, I persistently fought the urge to jump out of the car just to know what that would feel like at 60 mph.

Despite all the dangers, I had managed to avoid a premature ankle-biter death, but it wasn't for lack of trying.

The unlocked cabinet under our kitchen sink contained enough deadly poisons to wipe out a small New England village.

One morning, I crawled on my hands and knees across the kitchen floor, pulled open the cabinet door, and stared wide-eyed at the hidden treasure chest of bright red, green, and yellow cans and bottles containing *Drano* drain crystals, *Spic and Span* floor cleaner, *Easy-Off* oven spray. The choice of toxic toys, snacks, and drinks riveted me—a toddler's viper brew of quaternary ammonium, butoxyethanol, methoxydiglycol, and other unpronounceable delicacies.

A dazzling crimson package of steel wool Brillo Pads caught

my eye. I chewed a corner off the box, reached inside, and plucked out what appeared to be a pillow-shaped biscuit of gleaming shredded wheat.

As I raised the scrub pad toward my mouth, my stupefied peepers shifted to a radiant chartreuse bottle of Mr. Clean standing under the drain trap as if he single-handedly held up the cast-iron sink. His warm smile beckoned me. His sparkling golden earring charmed me. His bushy, cloud-white eyebrows, t-shirt, and bulging crossed arms entranced me. I imagined that he had placed the magic potion under the sink just for me. One swig from the bottle and I, too, could be Mr. Clean.

As I fidgeted with the metal cap, the toilet flushed in the small washroom off the kitchen. Footsteps. My mother, Mrs. Clean, caught me red-handed. She yelled in her thick Brooklyn accent, "Philip, put that baht'ul down this instant! Nevva evva go in that cabinet again! And don't ask me why. It's becawse I told ya so!"

A simple child-proof latch might have kept me from consuming the cabinet full of deadly chemical cleaners. But the child safety lock wouldn't be invented for decades. Until then, preventing dangerous behavior amounted to second-chance threats from my mother. Her warnings always got my attention, including my favorite. "Go to your room, missta! The *next* time you shoot your brutha in the face, you'll nevva see yaw sling-shot again!"

I still can't shake my most traumatic childhood memory. I was around two years old when the eight-tentacled beast held me down in my crib. Try as I might, the octopus was too strong, too diabolical to release me from its stranglehold.

The second floor of our house featured a peaked-roofed room above the front porch, not much larger than a lunch box.

This tucked-away space was called "the coop." This was the room that Lou and Dot Caragol chose for me to sleep in—a nursery named after a barnyard shack used to cage chatterbox chicks.

The coop housed a small prison, a wooden crib framed with bars to prevent a pipsqueak jailbreak. To further protect me from climbing out of the crib and plunging to certain death, my mom took the extra precaution of strapping me into the crib with the notorious toddler harness, an ingenious device resembling an eight-legged octopus recommended by Dr. Spock, the famous pedia-quack of the baby boom era.

The revolutionary child restraining system was most likely developed in a dank basement by a do-it-yourselfer whose particular passion was the study of medieval torture contraptions. After experimenting with inventions such as toddler shackles and the toddler rack, he successfully marketed a harness that offered superior restraining properties without all the heavy, cumbersome dungeon chains, ropes, padlocks, and pulleys.

The toddler harness had several attractive selling features going for it. First, it was based on proven centuries-old technology that no one questioned. The same basic harness design that allowed oxen to pull covered wagons for hundreds of miles across the frontier prairie, and enabled Clydesdales to tow the Budweiser beer wagon across a TV screen, would certainly provide the strength and reliability required to effectively restrain a helpless child.

Secondly, the toddler harness made child restraint as easy as dressing a mental institution patient in a straightjacket:

1. Slip the one-size-fits-all, easy-to-wash canvas vest on your kid.

2. Secure the vest by tightening the belt straps up the back.

3. Tie the vest's elastic straps around the bars of the crib and

squeeze the convenient button snap at the end of each strap for a secure hold.

In just minutes, even the most mechanically challenged mom could have her kid safely strapped down for the night. She could go to bed, assured that the harness straps were long enough to allow her rug rat to roll from side to side or even to stand up and peer over the top of the crib. But they were also short enough to prevent Junior from bungee jumping over the side.

No child in the brief history of the toddler harness had ever broken out of its tentacled grasp. Certainly, many mini Houdinis had attempted to escape from the infernal vest. Yet none had succeeded. Until...

One restless night I sat up in the crib with a load in my diapers and a crappy attitude. I wanted to escape at any cost. I stood up and walked like a drunken sailor toward the front of the crib. After two small steps, I tilted forward at a 45-degree angle as if bracing myself against a gale force Nor'easter. The taut tentacles stretched to the back of the crib. The limit of their maximum elasticity would not cut me the slack needed to take one more step.

White-hot rage rose inside me like molten magma in the bulging cone of a soon-to-erupt baby volcano. This was my room, my crib. I was a stinking mess, and I wanted out. Damn the damn tentacles. This was war.

I called on every muscle in my young body to push forward. I teetered on one foot, lifted the other tiny foot off the slippery plastic mattress cover, and strained to take another step.

BRRRANG. The high-tension straps recoiled and lurched me off the mattress. I shot backward through the air straight into the headboard. I stood up and, this time, ran. BRRRANG. Crawled. BRRRANG.

I bellied up to the side of the crib and used the added power of leverage to pull myself along the length of the top rail.

I didn't realize it at the time, but this was my first experiment in physics. Hand by hand and step by grueling step brought me beyond my farthest point so far. I had passed the 50-yard line of the mattress. The end zone was in sight. I had no idea what I was going to do when I reached it, but damn it, I was going to get there.

My struggle against the harness straps felt agonizing. I sweated. I grunted. I yelled toddler obscenities. "RAHHHHHH! ARRRRRRRR! GAAAAAAAA!"

The foul-mouthed, high-pitched kiddo curses awakened my mother in the middle of the night. As I took my last strenuous step to the far end of the crib, strangling the corner post with my bare hands, I felt myself being picked up and unsnapped from the tentacled monster.

Momma came to my rescue, which is more than I can say for the harness designed to save my life. She stuffed it in the trashcan and never made me wear it again.

In that one brief, intense struggle with the crib octopus, I learned an early life lesson: When you want something bad enough, nothing can hold you back, especially when a friend comes along to snap you out of your misery.

❦ 2 ❧
SCATTERBRAIN-ITIS

"When my kids become wild and unruly, I use a nice, safe playpen.
When they're finished, I climb out."
- **Erma Bombeck**

The basic concept of *think before you act* never entered my sputtering mind when I was a kid. Like an entire herd of stampeding bulls in a china shop, I left a trail of mayhem that exhausted my parents, teachers, and pretty much anyone else caught in my higgledy-piggledy path.

Actions that seemed natural to me weren't. I didn't understand why my folks got so upset when I unscrewed a heavy wood block pedal from my tricycle and threw it into the windshield of a passing motorist in front of our house. They didn't understand why I thought it was a good idea to feed salads smothered in artery-clogging Russian dressing to our pet box turtles, Turty One through Turty Turteen, who all prematurely bit the dust inside their shells in a tragic series of heart attacks.

I didn't learn until my fifties that the source of my lack of focus had an actual clinical name. ADHD. The closest early diagnosis came from my kindergarten teacher, Mrs. Goldberg, when I was five. I had just flunked "Structured Schedules" when she broke the dreaded news about my mental condition to my folks during a parent-teacher conference. "I'm sorry to report, Mr. and Mrs. Caragol...that your son is severely scatter-brained."

In retrospect, I can't blame Mrs. Goldberg for concluding that I was as impulsive and flittering as a squirrel.

On one occasion, I drifted off to the cloakroom while my classmates were busy making paper airplanes at the arts and crafts table. Who wouldn't? There were so many fabulous jackets and hats to try on that it might as well have been the children's clothing department at Macy's.

I was particularly enamored with Billy Martin's Air Force bomber jacket and matching flap cap. When Mrs. Goldberg called out, "Philip Caragol, where have you gone to now?" I took that as my stage cue.

I strutted back into the classroom on an imaginary fashion runway, pivoted in a dramatic circle at the crafts table, and paused to allow the crowd of kindergarteners to ooo and ahh. In reality, the only ooos and ahhs were my own wails when Mrs. Goldberg swatted my butt for disrupting her critical life lesson in paper plane making.

Concentrating during craft time continued to be a mighty struggle, especially when Mrs. Goldberg decided we were ready to take on a project that I will forever remember as The Bloody Maypole Dance.

We sat in a circle on the classroom floor. She explained, "Listen up, children. I have exciting news. We are going to celebrate May Day this year with a special performance for your mommies called The Maypole Dance."

She lost me at, "Listen up, children."

The next thing I knew, she dragged a tall wooden pole in a Christmas tree stand out of the closet and told us to gather

around it. "The Maypole Dance is an ancient tradition celebrated by boys and girls just like you for hundreds of years."
She failed to mention that the dance was a pagan fertility ritual
performed by boy and girl Druids around a pole resembling an
erect penis. "We'll attach red and white streamers to the top of
the pole and dance in an inner and outer circle until we braid
the pole and then dance in the opposite direction to unwind
the ribbons."

I stared at Mrs. Goldberg with my mouth wide open, drool
running down my chin, my mind spinning hopelessly out of
control. She had unknowingly overloaded my brain with not
one but six instructions in a babbling run-on sentence that
made no sense. She stared back. "Questions?"

I didn't know where to start. Forcing us to perform anything
as complex as a Maypole Dance was the worst idea in the
history of bad ideas.

Over the next week, we went to work making decorations
for the Druid phallus waltz. Mrs. Goldberg showed us how to
cut the long ribbons that we'd use for streamers attached to the
maypole. She measured a strand of red ribbon using a yardstick, lopped off a nine-foot section with scissors, and asked,
"Who wants to cut the next streamer?" I was the only one who
raised a hand. "Me! Me! Me! Me! Pick me!" She picked mini-
debutant Jeanie Alban, a suck-up teacher's pet if there ever
was one.

We divided into groups of four to cut the rest of the 18
ribbons, one for each puny pagan dancer. My group included
three other misfits: Susie Cornwall, a chronic bed wetter who
regularly peed on her blanket during naptime; Janie MacKen-
zie, a nearly blind girl whose heavy black eyeglasses constantly
slid down to the tip of her nose; and Guido Ferrara, a stout
schoolyard prizefighter known for his spring-loaded temper.

Janie ran her all-seeing hands over the work table, found
the roll of ribbon, and handed it to Susie. Susie measured and

marked a nine-foot length with a pencil. Guido held the ribbon on both sides of the mark. I wasn't paying attention and sliced off the tip of Guido's thumb with the scissors.

He shouted the first words I ever heard in Italian. "Fottuto idiota!" which I later learned meant, "You fucking idiot!"

Susie wet her plaid shorts.

Guido wrapped his thumb with a handkerchief and stuck it in my face. "I'll get you for this, Caragol. Better watch your back." I didn't know he meant it so literally.

On the day of the performance, as mothers claimed their seats around the Maypole, Guido cornered me in the cloakroom. While I checked out the season's spring wardrobe of the girls' bright pastel and bold-print jackets, Guido hung me on a coat hook and left me there. The protruding hook scraped my back and tore my shirt as I dangled above the floor, held up only by the shirt loop knotted around the hook.

After lots of air-kicking, the loop and a large swath of my shirt tore free. I heard the Irish jig music start and ran out of the cloakroom just in time to grab a streamer and take my place in the outer circle of the Maypole Dance.

A mob of moms packed the open classroom and applauded when we completed the first full dance around the pole. Seconds later, the applause faded.

I wondered why several mothers pointed at me and whispered something into each other's ears. I had worked so hard to grasp and master the dance moves that Mrs. Goldberg had taught us. My heart swelled with a new sense of accomplishment. I thought *All of my hard work was paying off! These people love me! I'm killing it right now! I'm a normal kid!*

In actuality, the only thing killed in the room was the festive mood. The parental appreciation Mrs. Goldberg hoped for had evaporated. The world-class dance of the Druids she had choreographed dissolved into a crime scene, starring the backstabbed Maypole kindergartener in the blood-stained white school shirt.

It was then that I discovered the true gift of Scatterbrain-itis. For better or worse, I possessed the superpower to scatter a roomful of mothers like rats in spring dresses jumping off the deck of a sinking preschool ship.

❦ 3 ❦
PLAYING DOCTOR: AN
IMMORALITY PLAY

"When I was born, I was so ugly the doctor slapped my mother."
- Rodney Dangerfield

Betwen the time when medieval doctors prescribed leeches and modern insurance companies became leeches, American families enjoyed a brief period of healthcare nirvana.

When I was born in the '50s, my parents paid the hospital $165 in cash for my delivery, plus a carefree seven-day vacation in a private room for my mom. This fabulous package deal also included three meals a day and a squad of nurses in crisp white caps and dresses standing by to rock me so Mom could rest. The only missing amenities were complimentary cocktails and hors d'oeuvres served by doting young Chippendale doctors.

These days, we're told to wait days, weeks, or months before a doctor will see us—unless it's a condition needing immediate medical attention, like accidentally sawing off an arm in the tool shed.

In that case, we can drive with our remaining arm to the

emergency room, where fifty other patients with missing limbs are also waiting to be seen by a doctor.

Compare that to a bygone practice known as the "house call." Too sick to go to the doctor's office? No worries. The family doctor came to your bedside at home, carrying a black leather bag filled with the essentials needed to diagnose and treat maladies such as bronchitis, hallucinatory fevers, childhood mumps, and chicken pox.

Our family doctor was an ex-WWII army medic. Tending to a serious sinus infection paled in comparison to sewing up chest wounds under gunfire on Omaha Beach.

Dr. Raymond Varino was a close friend of my father. We addressed him affectionately as Uncle Ray. He never failed us, including the time I bubbled up with what felt like the most severe case of poison ivy in human history.

The day before, my dad and I hopped in the car for a Sunday drive north to Connecticut. There we were, father and five-year-old son, having the time of our lives on a crisp autumn afternoon. We meandered on country roads through leafy tunnels of red, yellow, and orange tree canopies while listening to the soothing melodies of Mantovani's Thousand Strings Orchestra on the car radio.

Dad packed a picnic of baloney and mayo sandwiches on white Wonder Bread and two bottles of Crush orange soda. We lunched by the side of a river on the front bench seat of our station wagon.

The baloney sandwich I scarfed down set off an emergency siren in my bowel region.

"Dad, I hafta go! But they-ah's no bathroom!"

My dad's advice was, "Go behind the bushes over there, Philly," pointing to a wall of scrub bushes by the river.

"But they-ah's no toilet pape-ah!"

"Just use some leaves," my father advised. "They'll do the job."

Off I ran, clinching my buttocks together like a small industrial vice. I rounded the bushes, dropped my pants, and let go of the most euphoric bowel movement of my young life. A Speedy Alka Seltzer TV jingle rang in my head. "*Plop plop, fizz fizz, oh what a relief it is!*"

I reached down, grabbed a pile of leaves in my pink palm, and wiped. Then I grabbed more leaves and wiped two more times to be sure I wouldn't soil my underwear. This selfless act would spare my mother from unnecessary extra work and nausea on laundry day.

The next morning, my hindquarters itched and burned like a 10-alarm fire. For that matter, so did my hands, wrists, ears, crotch, penis and armpits. I jumped out of bed and stripped off my Roy Rogers pajamas sporting cowboys on horseback lassoing cattle. "Mahhh-mahhh!"

Mom barreled into my bedroom, gobsmacked by the sight of my impish body covered in oozing yellowish blisters. I'd never heard the words *poison ivy* before. But that's the name of the leaves I used in place of toilet paper by the river.

The blooming blisters were not only ON my butt. They were IN my butt and everywhere else I touched, rubbed, or scratched with my hands, tainted with invisible poison ivy oil slicks.

Uncle Ray rushed to the house at my mom's request. He entered my room like Ray the Archangel to do battle with my boils. He opened his doctor's bag and snapped a pair of light green surgical gloves on his hands.

His alert eyes darted back and forth over his black reading glasses as he performed a full-body examination, including my dinky penis, now swollen to roughly the size of a baby elephant trunk.

He ushered Mom into the hall and whispered in her ear. Their conversation looked serious. Was I going to die from ivy poisoning? She nodded with the frantic acknowledgments of a dashboard bobblehead. She understood what she had to do to save my life. He wrote a prescription. Mom clutched it in her trembling fist.

Uncle Ray came back to my bedside and patted my head with his gloved hand. On the way out, he turned and said, "We'll get you in ship shape in no time." I appreciated his reassurance, even though *ship shape* sounded like a stretch coming from a doctor who served in the army.

One bottle of steroid pills and three bottles of pink calamine skin lotion later, the rash, itching, and oozing gradually disappeared. Uncle Ray hadn't fibbed after all. In two weeks, I felt ship shape again and returned to my regular activities—plus a new one that launched my prestigious first-grade medical career.

Uncle Ray's medical prowess made a big impression on me. So much so that I asked my parents to buy a doctor's bag for my birthday. Sure, I was only five, but why should that prevent me from becoming a world-renowned physician?

All I needed were the proper tools to heal the sick and help cripples walk again. I envisioned myself as the miraculous new healer of Aspen Street who would rush to the homes of infirm neighbors, just like Uncle Ray did.

Birthday wish granted. I ripped the cowboy wrapping paper off the gift box. I almost cried. My very own *Little Family Doctor* bag appeared in my nimble surgical hands, the harbinger of a budding medical career.

This was not the base model of *Little Family Doctor*. My parents went all-out and bought the deluxe version, quite possibly to ease my father's guilt. His advice to wipe myself with poison ivy became the catalyst for a prestigious gift received only by the finest medical professionals.

I pressed the shiny silver release buttons of the locks on top of the black fake leather bag. They sprang open with satisfying *whap whaps*, inviting me to peer inside. I gently pulled the child-sized handles apart. The scent of fresh medical supplies filled my nostrils with tingling anticipation.

I splayed out the left and right compartments. The reveal presented what I can only describe as the essentials for launching a distinguished medical practice:

• Official Doctor's Shingle for my medical office, formerly a storage closet under the living room stairs;

• Official Doctor's Certificate, suitable for framing and hanging in said office to assure patients of my stellar credentials;

• Hospital Record Sheets to document my human patients' and pet hamster's names, ages, heart rates, temperatures, symptoms, and recommended treatments;

• *Professional Secrets for the Play Doctor*, my go-to doctor's handbook chockfull of medical white papers concerning the diagnosis and treatment of both common and rare ailments such as Candy Colitis;

• Round Examination Glasses with center magnifying lenses, ideal for the detailed inspection of suspicious warts, moles, and freckles;

• Peppermint Pill Envelopes filled by the revered Playland pharmacy;

• Glass Vials with screw caps, useful for protecting biopsies, blood samples, and boogers from contaminants such as pencil eraser crumbs;

• Doctor's Circular Head-Strap Mirror with a hole in the center to examine patients while staring into their crusty nostrils, inflamed throats, and wax-balled ears;

• Playland Hospital sterilized cotton balls, gauze, and adhesive bandages for the application of ointments and sealing of lethal wounds caused by the careless use of pocketknives;

- Blood Pressure Cuff complete with squeaking inflatable bulb and spinning arrow doubling as both a blood pressure gauge and search-and-rescue compass;
- Authentic Hospital Stethoscope made of genuine plastic from the island of Japan, boasting the world's highest plastic production output and lowest rate of cardiac arrests.

I could hardly wait to try out my new doctor bag and medical knowledge on any patient, no matter the number of legs. I carefully looped the handles of my doctor bag over the handles of my tricycle and set out in search of my first patient.

As fate would have it, the patient exited her home a few doors down and walked toward me on the sidewalk. Regina Yoder and I were the same age, friends who played together at both of our homes. I greeted her with a professional smile, becoming of our town's newest young doctor.

"Good afta-noon, Regina."

"Hi, Phil. What are you doing today?"

"I'm happy you asked, Regina. Today is my birthday. Wanna see my new doc-tah bag?"

She was intrigued. I opened the bag and showed her its contents, taking care to describe every item and its purpose. Little did I know that Regina also wanted to enter the medical profession.

"Let's play doctor!" she offered.

"I, really, really hoped you'd say that, Regina! Let's go to my house!"

She hopped on the back of the tricycle, and I pedaled us to the front of my house. I suddenly realized that my office wasn't ready yet. Mom still had it packed with storage boxes of old clothes, the Hoover vacuum cleaner, and my dad's golf clubs covered with cobwebs.

Scanning the porch, I realized that the wide brick wall surrounding the front stoop would provide an adequate substitute for an examination table.

Stoop, derived from the Dutch term *stoep*, meant a small porch. It may have looked small to a full-grown adult, but it looked as big as the landing deck of an aircraft carrier to Regina and me. We were three and a half feet tall, and everything loomed large from where we stood.

It was late May and unseasonably warm. I offered to go first and play the patient while Regina assumed the duties of doctor. We were just kids. Getting naked didn't raise either of our eyebrows. She'd taken baths with her brothers, so seeing me in all my glory was no big surprise.

I stripped off my striped T-shirt, khaki shorts, underwear, socks, and Buster Brown shoes as cars drove by slowly, and the mailman skipped our house.

Dr. Regina plugged the stethoscope into her ears. She started at the top and worked her way down, listening to my forehead, clavicle, nipples, heart, elbows, stomach, hips, thighs, knees, calves, ankles, and feet.

She asked what the cuff was for. I reached for my *Professional Secrets for the Play Doctor* handbook. I mostly read children's books at that point, filled with more pictures than words. Instructions on the *How to Check Blood Pressure* page were beyond my reading level and attention span. Fortunately, the page displayed an illustration of the blood pressure cuff in action. I showed her the drawing and said, "Just folla diss."

Unbeknownst to me, Regina was an advanced reader. She wrapped the cuff around my bicep, pumped the bulb (squeak, squeak, squeak), and placed the listening end of the stethoscope over a bulging vein in my arm. The arrow on the blood pressure dial spun in circles and stopped on true north. With absolute confidence, she informed me, "You're going to live."

I put my clothes back on, and Regina stripped down, bucknaked on our front porch. The mailman hesitantly walked past us a second time. Another car drove by. A grandma behind the wheel stared out the window, thunderstruck, her mouth wide open in shock.

It occurred to me that Regina was serious future doctor material. So, I followed her examination protocol. When I got to her quizzical spot below the hips, I paused. Unlike Regina, who had seen her brothers naked, I had never seen my older sister naked, nor my mother, nor anyone of the female gender.

It became obvious to me that Regina was missing something.

As she lay on the exam table of the stoop, I looked down at her organ-less region, perplexed. Apparently, there were some physical differences between boys and girls that I was not aware of. Differences any doctor worth his or her salt should know.

I had all kinds of questions and asked, "Regina, how come yaw..."

The high-pitched creak of our heavy wooden front door ripping open cut me off in midsentence. My mother yelled at us in her Brooklyn accent, "Philip! De-ah Gawd! Regina put yaw clothes on! That's so IMMORAL!!!!"

Regina and I didn't have the slightest idea what Mom meant by "immoral," but whatever it meant wasn't good. Regina put her clothes back on, walked home, and we never played doctor again.

Unfortunately, that only left one available patient. My pet rodent, Jake, passed his hamster wheel cardio stress test with flying colors.

❦ 4 ❦
REVENGE OF THE CAMPERS

Hello Muddah. Hello Faddah.
Here I am at Camp Grenada
Camp is very entertaining
And they say we'll have some fun if it stops raining.
- Alan Sherman

Directly after I graduated from kindergarten, my parents dropped my brother and me off at Pinecrest Dunes summer camp, and I watched them drive away down a sandy road into oblivion.

Summer camp occupied a sprawling landmass not dissimilar to the size of a small Latin American country. Miles of shoreline on the Long Island Sound marked the far boundary of the camp, an ideal place for children to cool off and potentially drown if the coed lifeguards ogled each other instead of watching the kids flailing out in the water.

A dozen whitewashed wooden cabins were scattered across the dunes. They housed 100 campers from ages five to 16. The boys' and girls' cabins were strategically positioned on opposite sides of the camp. Boys were strictly prohibited from going over to the girls' camp, and vice versa. But the older kids always managed to sneak over to the other side, as oversexed teenagers will do.

My group was the youngest, kids aged eight and under. While older groups were given cool names like the Cobras, ours was named the Tadpoles. Really? I could barely even swim yet, and as far as I knew, I didn't have a tail. As camp names go, my group was a case study in "Early Child Humiliation Development."

On my second day of camp, I had no idea when or where I was supposed to be at any given time. Much to my dismay, summer camp (like kindergarten) was all about "Structured Schedules," posted on the trunk of a towering oak tree in the center of camp.

A large corkboard bolted into the tree displayed the day's activities. Each activity was listed by group, time, location, and the name of the counselor supervising the activity. Each day, the sheet of activities changed. This complex system of multiple shifting variables might have worked if they had the decency to start camp with a full-week orientation seminar in "Time Management for The Wee Ones Who Have No Concept of Time."

With no treatment for my Scatterbrain-itis, I wandered aimlessly around camp, day after day, stopping wherever an activity attracted my limited attention span.

I pounded tin squares into ashtrays for my parents when I should have been at the archery range learning how to defend myself against warrior tribes still hiding in the woods of Eastern Long Island.

I ducked into the camp director's log house to play with his two giant St. Bernard dogs when I was supposed to be at the stables learning how to ride a pony (which would have come in handy in the unlikely event I won the role of Paul Revere in a future school play).

I never showed up on time for swim lessons at the lake, but the counselors took roll call and knew when I went missing. They eventually tracked me down thanks to the public address system that boomed throughout the camp.

"Attention all staff! This is an important announcement. Tadpole, Philip Caragol, wearing a green striped T-shirt and blue paisley swim trunks, went missing. Please find him and bring him immediately to the swimming area at the lake."

Whenever I did wander toward the lake, it wasn't long before I ran off to chase a squirrel that caught my eye, and then a frog, a caterpillar, a seagull, a worm, a gust of swirling dust, and so on.

I bounced from one thing to another so often that, on skit night, my cabin mates cast me in the role of Skippy, the ping-pong ball.

Mr. Whalen was the founder, owner, and director of the camp. He was a dead ringer for Teddy Roosevelt and in amazing shape for a man in his early 60s. While only 5-foot, 3 inches tall, he was an imposing figure with round gold-rimmed glasses, a handlebar mustache, broad shoulders, barrel chest, thin waist, muscular biceps, and the bulging legs of a pro football player.

Nicknamed "Derr" for reasons unknown to me, Mr. Whalen was a world-class Olympic swimmer in his youth and flew Navy seaplanes in the Pacific in World War II. After the war, New York newspapers reported the story about his crash in his private seaplane.

The twin-propellor engines failed, and he crashed into the frigid February waters of Long Island Sound. Fogged in and with no boats in sight, Derr stripped down, swam a mile to shore, crawled across the dunes to the nearest house, and became a local living legend.

He treated every camper, including my brother Richie and me, to a flight in his pontooned seaplane docked on the lake. Fortunately, no one had told me about the crash. Otherwise, I might have thought twice about climbing up into the four-passenger cockpit.

Richie and I sat in the back seat and could barely see out the windshield when Mr. Whalen started the engines. The roar of the motors sent chills down my spine as we sped across the lake. I peeked out the side window and noticed we were skipping across the water straight toward a gray-shingled summer home on the lake. I prayed, "De-ah Jesus, please don't take me now." Mr. Whalen yelled, "Hold on, boys! It's lift-off time!"

We soared over the house just as a man on the porch raised his middle finger and waved at us. I admired lake people. They were so friendly.

The real thrill was yet to come. High above the Sound, Mr. Whalen cut the engines and dropped the plane into a nosedive. We screamed. The white-capped waves below us came closer and closer. G-forces pulled our rigid bodies forward, our startled faces planted into the back of the front seats.

In the last seconds before we plunged to our deaths, the engines kicked in again. The plane leveled out just above the whitecaps. We glided onto the surface, touched down, and flew back up into the sky at a speed that can best be described as "puking velocity."

My brother and I bunked in the same knotty pine cabin with ten other boys. Our ornery counselor, Filbert, slept in an adjoining private bedroom.

At my age, everyone over the age of 12 looked old. Filbert

may have been 17 or 27. Either way, he was in a foul mood most of the time and equally foul-mouthed. Filbert treated us as his personal camper slaves.

"You, shit for brains! Clean the toilets!" "You, dwarf boy! Make my bed!"

"You, zit face! Fetch me a chocolate bar and Coke from the snack shack!"

I couldn't decide whether Filbert was a direct descendant of Hitler, Rasputin, or Jack the Ripper. No matter his ancestry, Filbert was a nut, ready to crack.

His rotund physique bore a striking resemblance to Jabba the Hutt in human form. Descending rolls of fat jiggled like a stack of truck tires from his quadruple-D man boobs down to the bulging butter pouch below his belt.

I had never met his mother, but I felt deep compassion for her. Labor and delivery must have been excruciating. Based on Filbert's adult size, it was not a stretch to imagine him as a freakishly giant fetus along the magnitude of a first-prize watermelon at the summer harvest festival, extracted by the Jaws of Life from the car wreck that was his mother's womb.

Filbert's negative body image probably played a major role in his nasty attitude. It would be years before we fully grasped the enormous effect of low self-esteem on mental health. In the meantime, we and our cabin mates behaved and did as we were told. None of us wanted to face the wrath of Filbert the Crotchety Counselor. Unfortunately, two of us did.

One night before lights out, my brother snuck out of the cabin. He stood in the dark outside the screen window next to our bunkbed and waited. I had just finished brushing my teeth in the boys' bathroom. As I walked toward our bunk, a ghost appeared outside the window. It didn't occur to me that the ghost was my brother, who pressed his ghoulishly illuminated face against the window screen with a flashlight under his chin.

I screamed and ran to the other end of the cabin, as far

away from the ghost as possible. The only place to hide was in a toilet stall. I slammed and locked the swinging stall door behind me, shaking with terror. That's when I noticed the pool of blood.

Somewhere along my mad dash to the lavatory, I rammed my big toe into a jagged splinter sticking out of a floorboard. The splinter, roughly the size of several matchsticks, lodged under my big toenail. I screamed again. Filbert wobbled in and banged on the stall door just as Richie arrived, shining his flashlight in my face.

"Oh man, you twat-heads are in for a lotta trouble," Filbert growled, his jowls quivering like bowls of Jell-O. He pointed at my brother. "You, Spawn of Satan! What did you do to him? Tell me the truth, or there'll be hell to pay. A hell you'll remember 'til the goddamn day you burn there!"

I must admit, Filbert did have a talent for clear, persuasive language.

Richie and I confessed the details of our ghostly encounter. Filbert ordered Richie to sit on the toilet until he and I returned from the nurse's office. That worked out for my nervous brother, who was about to drop a 10-megaton bomb in his shorts.

I couldn't walk, so Filbert flung me over his shoulder like a sack of potatoes, and off we went to seek medical attention. He breathed so heavily from overexertion that I thought he might also need medical attention.

After the nurse yanked the splinter out with needle-nose pliers and bandaged my toe, Filbert dragged me back to the cabin. As ordered, Richie still sat on the toilet seat looking pale and sheepish, yet relieved now that he had released the bomb.

Filbert left us for a few seconds and marched back into the bathroom, holding a second flashlight. "Come with me, you twerps!" Then he yelled, "Lights out!" Bobbie Radcliff slept below the light switch. He reached up and plunged the bunkroom into darkness.

Filbert led us out behind the cabin, guiding us to who knows where with beams of light from his and Richie's flashlights. The bright lights attracted swarms of tiny translucent gnats, soon to become Filbert's flying instruments of torture.

We stopped on the dunes far behind the cabin. Filbert handed the flashlights to us. A wicked smile crept across his face as if he had just given us booby-trapped birthday presents. "Hold those under your chin, you geniuses. And don't move a muscle until I come back."

The flashlights blinded us. Or maybe it was the gnats. Probably both. The tiny buzzing fiends nibbled at our eyelids. No matter how tightly we shut our eyes, the gnats worked their way in. For the first time, nature revealed to us an ugly truth. We were both hyper-allergic to gnat bites.

Our eyes began to swell and itch. Rubbing them only made the itching worse. Bumps on the undersides of our eyelids scratched our eyes like rough sandpaper. And that wasn't the worst part.

Gnats zipped up our nostrils. They flew into our ear canals like fighter plane squadrons. We inhaled entire gnat families and villages into our mouths, throats, and lungs. They nested and hatched biting babies on our exposed flesh. They celebrated an early gnats Thanksgiving, a glorious day of feasting on sweet camper meat.

In a word, we were the childhood victims of a *Gnatastrophe*.

We lost track of how long Filbert left us out there being eaten alive. When he returned, we could barely see or hear him. Our eyes were swollen shut. The high-pitched buzz of gnats partying on our eardrums eviscerated our ability to hear. In a single night, Richie and I became the Helen Kellers of Pinecrest Dunes.

Filbert finally returned. We formed a human chain back to

the cabin by holding onto one another's belt sloops. Filbert took the front position, the obese leading the blind.

To avoid camp prosecution for his actions, Filbert hid the evidence.

He sentenced Richie and me to cabin sequestration until our puffy, blistered faces showed no signs of gnat torture.

Those free days gave Richie plenty of time to concoct a brilliant plan of revenge.

Filbert showered in the boys' bathhouse every Wednesday at precisely 2 p.m. He scheduled his shower carefully at a time when all male campers and counselors were at the beach.

The open shower bay afforded no privacy.

The last thing Filbert wanted was to be seen naked. Word would spread about his whalelike proportions. Girls would giggle, and boys would whisper when he passed through the buffet line in the dining hall, heaping piles of lasagna and mashed potatoes onto his plate.

Filbert's greatest fear was also his greatest weakness.

My big brother preyed on that weakness. He mapped out a plot so simple and diabolical that even a seven-year-old camper could pull it off.

While Filbert lathered up in the open shower bay, Richie hid behind a nearby tree and pointed his weapon—a Polaroid camera he borrowed from Tommy DiAngelo, a rich kid in our cabin whose dad ran a prostitution ring for a Long Island mob family.

Click. Polaroid #1.

Click. Polaroid #2.

By the time Richie finished firing his instant camera, we had a dozen crystal-clear Polaroid photos of Filbert in all of his corpulent glory.

We placed one photo and a signed bribery note on his bed:

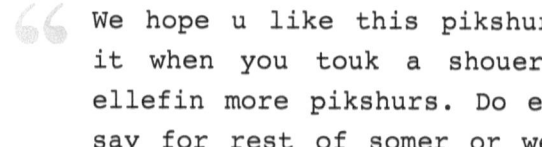

> We hope u like this pikshur. We maid
> it when you touk a shouer. We have
> ellefin more pikshurs. Do everting we
> say for rest of somer or we show yor
> pikshurs to hole girl camp. We r not
> kindling.

When Filbert returned from the showers, he jiggled into his bedroom and closed the door. We expected to hear him swear like a sailor and throw things against the wall.

Surprisingly, he was as quiet as a church mouse, even when we made him clean the toilets, make our beds, and fetch treats for us from the snack shack.

They tasted better than ever when served with a generous portion of boyhood justice.

5

ATTACK OF THE APE WOMAN

"It wasn't airplanes. It was Beauty killed the Beast."
- Carl Denham, King Kong's captor

T he fear of animals runs in my family. Don't get me wrong. Pets are great companions. Over the years, we've raised three Basset Hounds, two Labrador Retrievers, two cats, one rabbit, one goldfish, and 17 mice (compliments of two females that turned out to be a helpless female and Don Juan de Rodent). I'm talking about a fear of animal types you wouldn't walk on a leash, wash in the bathtub, or roll around with on the hall carpet. Lions. Tigers. Bears. Boars. Wolves. Rhinos. And, especially, half-human gorillas.

My fear of large predatory beasts is more a fear of the unknown, made acute by the complete absence of exotic animals where I grew up in the dense suburbs of Long Island. This was a place where "the wide-open spaces" measured 10 feet wide. We called them driveways.

In our neighborhood of brick houses lined up in rows like dominos on cookie-cutter lots, the only wild animal I ever saw was a lone operator, a solitary gray squirrel. The furry chestnut hoarder was as elusive as Big Foot.

One kid on my block armed with a Red Rider BB gun, Bobby Mackaley, captured a rare photo of the furry phantom flicking his bushy tail while descending a tree head first. The scamp was fast, cunning, camouflaged to blend into the gray New York landscape, and nearly impossible to shoot.

I never saw two squirrels together at the same time, a clear sign that the entire species had died off except for this one courageous super squirrel.

Our army of pint-sized urban hunters was no match for the legendary creature that outwitted us and survived mostly on chestnuts and midnight snacks of coffee grounds, egg shells, and dried macaroni-and-cheese clumps on the ground around our backyard trash cans.

Despite his celebrity status in our neighborhood, the super squirrel and the rabies he carried were about as frightening to me as a doe-eyed Chihuahua.

No, he would never burrow his way into our basement, scurry up the stairs, sneak into my room, hide under the bed, and tear me to shreds with his acorn-cracking claws when I turned off the light. He was, after all, a squirrel—a threat about as imposing as a glove puppet.

A beast that could really do me in had to be much, much more ferocious than that. It had to be hungry for the flesh of a second grader. Armed with yellow razor-sharp fangs. Built with bulging muscles capable of splitting open my skull like a termite nest.

But, to be truly frightening, an animal had to be much, much more than even that. It had to be part wild beast and part human.

Only then could it knock on the door, trick my parents into allowing it to come into the house, transform itself into something hideous, sneak under the bed, and rip me apart in the all-alone blackness of my bedroom.

I met her at age seven on a stormy Saturday afternoon. Richie and I saw her come into our basement through our flickering black-and-white television screen.

Her name was Ape Woman.

She was an attractive young secretary who worked for a mad scientist. He developed a serum derived from gorillas that he proceeded to test on a human subject. His eccentric theory was that the serum would give his assistant the apish strength of a Silverback gorilla without altering her physical appearance.

After the injection, the poor woman (locked in a cage dangled from the laboratory ceiling) transformed before my eyes into a frenetic, cage-banging ape.

The time-lapsed film showed spikes of black hair sprouting up on her bulging head, arms, and legs. Every inch of her body that was legally allowed to be shown to the public during the Eisenhower Administration was displayed in hair-raising detail.

Her mouthful of orthodontically aligned white-chicklet teeth became a gaping hellhole of man-eating fangs dripping with drool. Her demure ski-slope nose collapsed into a flat mound of flared nostril Naugahyde. Inflated muscles ripped her secretarial suit into rags of virgin wool, revealing a figure so powerful she could single-handedly pummel an entire precinct of New York's finest.

She bent open the cage bars, leaped to the floor, strangled the professor, and escaped. That was the final straw that broke the monkey's back. The floodgates burst open. I peed my pants.

It was not a stoppable trickle. I experienced the Boulder Dam deluge of all bladder bursts. I peed my dungarees with firehose fury, soaked down to the drain gutters of my rolled-up cuffs.

Drenched pillows on the couch expanded like cartoon marshmallows. The braided oval rug squished, as did our miniature Collie, Rusty, who slept at my feet.

The only missing ingredient would have been a National Weather Service bulletin, "Attention! This is an extreme flood alert for all coastal areas on the Eastern seaboard. A pisser of a wave is due to strike at any moment or before the next scene in *Ape Woman*."

Ape Woman escaped. No one knew it except the murdered scientist, my brother, and me. She would kill us to protect herself from capture and a seat in the electric chair. I knew it to be true, and no one could convince me otherwise, including my mother.

Just when Ape Woman went missing (and schlepped her way to our house), Mom called downstairs, "Philip. Time to take yuh nap."

I thought she would go away if I ignored her. Unfortunately, she was a persistent German woman of unchangeable rules and schedules.

She called to me again, louder. "Philip. Did yuh he-ah me? It's time to come up for yuh nap."

Hoping that not replying would save me from having to go up to my room—WHERE APE WOMAN WAS WAITING FOR ME—I sat perfectly still in my soggy wet pants without saying a word. That was a mistake.

My mother expected me upstairs—now. Since I didn't come up, she called out again, louder. "Philip, if yuh not up he-ah by the time I count to three, yull be sorry! One (short stream of pee)...Two (down to the last drop)...Three (empty)."

She meant business. I heard her thick-heeled shoes clip-clop down the dark green linoleum stairs. I opened my eyes and looked up at Momma the Giant, her nose scrunched up, panning her head left and right like an oscillating fan.

The odor of my couch deluge had wafted into her overly-developed German nose. In her Edith Bunker Brooklyn accent, she asked my brother and me, "Boys. What is that awwwwful smell?"

I spilled my guts.

"Momma, I couh'nt help it," I cried. "I peed my pants on account of the Ape Woman escaped and nobody knows where she is but me and Richie and SHE'S COMIN' TO GET US and not only that but I know, I know, I know she's awlready up in my room RIGHT NOW and she's gonna kill me and EAT US UP. Oh please, oh please, don't make me go up they-ah. Oh please, momma!"

Let me say that Mom was the kindest, sweetest person I have ever known. I just picked a bad day to wet the couch at nap time.

She marched me up two flights of stairs to my bedroom, stopping on the way to pick up a yardstick from the broom closet in the kitchen. I warned her, "If we-ah gonna beat away Ape Woman, yaw gonna need a bigga stick!"

She flung open my bedroom door and asked me to get down on my knees with her to look under the bed. Mom whipped the yardstick under the mattress left to right, right to left, up and down, down and up. "Do yuh see any Ape Woman unduh he-ah?"

I screeched, "No! She's in the CLOSET!"

My mom led me by the hand to the closet and waved her ape-smacking yardstick back and forth under the neatly organized hangers of pressed shirts and trousers. "Do yuh see any Ape Woman unduh he-ah?" she asked.

"No! She's sneaky! She's nevva where ya look! She moves around! She's hidin' unduh the bed, and when we look, she'll sneak out again and run back to the closet! Waaaaaaaaaaaaaah!" The final thread of my mother's patience snapped. "Philip, there IS no Ape Woman!"

She slipped off my wet clothes, cleaned me with a wet face cloth, and dressed me in a fresh set of warm pajamas.

I crawled under the covers, pulled them over my head, and prayed, convinced that my last afternoon alive had arrived 80 years early.

One hour later, I awoke, relieved and thankful. Momma the Giant had chased away Ape Woman, toddled down to the laundry room with my wet pants in her arms, and quietly cleaned up the flood damage in the basement.

She never uttered a word of resentment or expected a word of thanks. That was not a mistake. That was love. That was Momma.

6

MOM TORE UP JAYNE MANSFIELD

"I've got the strangest build. It's big in the hips, small in the waist, and I've got these enormous...shoulders."
- Jayne Mansfield

Like my brothers and sister before me, I attended Catholic elementary school at Our Lady of Victory, two blocks and 100 tightly packed houses up the street. On my walk home in the third grade one chilly fall afternoon, I skipped down the sidewalk, kicking fallen leaves, when a black spit-polished stretch limousine backed out of a neighbor's driveway.

I had never seen a sedan approximately the length of a nuclear submarine. The limo just kept coming and coming out of the driveway. At one point, I wondered whether the front end was actually in our town or miles away, backing out of some faraway parking garage.

The front passenger door finally reached the sidewalk. The limo stopped, blocking my path. I saw the worried expression on my young, freckled face reflected in the window, tinted black so no one could see the passengers inside.

My Italian friends warned me about the mafia. The limo, the tinted glass, it all wreaked of goombahs capable of pulling out my cuticles with vice-grips or re-adjusting my nose with brass knuckles.

When I turned to back away, the window rolled down. Much to my surprise, the passenger was a spectacularly attractive dreamboat in a mink coat whom I later discovered was the actress Jayne Mansfield.

At the time, she was right up there with Marilyn Monroe in the Hollywood bleached blonde bombshell category. On a more personal level, she was my first encounter with the concepts of puberty and girlfriend.

Her amber eyes sparkled. A warm smile spread from the upturned corners of her lips. She introduced herself as "Jayne" and reached her velvety smooth, manicured hand out of the window. A flash of heat shot through me when her hand touched mine. I stared hypnotically into her glistening eyes. Something about her gaze drew us together as if a bridge had been built between the souls of two lonely strangers.

Jayne leaned toward me. Her angelic voice filled the still air between us. "Good afternoon, my sweet friend, would you like an autographed photo?" Unable to speak, I nodded *Yes, please*, not knowing what an autograph was or why a beautiful woman whom I had just met, who might become my first girlfriend, wanted to give me her picture.

It didn't matter what she asked of me. If Jayne said, "Would you like to smear this bowl of wet coffee grounds all over your face?" I would have enthusiastically replied, "Oh, yes, Miss Mansfield. I'd be honored."

She turned to the chauffeur, who wore a crisp black suit, matching cap, and leather gloves. He opened a small attaché case on the front seat and pulled out an 8" x 10" black and white glossy photo and a gold felt pen.

Jayne glanced up. A question formed around the curves of

her pursed lips. "Whose name should I write on the picture, baby doll?" I said, "Yaws." She giggled. "I mean, what's *your* name?" I said, "Phil." She penned something on the picture and handed it to me out the window. "Phil, you made my day. I'm so happy we met and hope we'll see each other again real soon."

I waved goodbye, lovesick and dumbstruck. She blew a farewell kiss. The limo drove away, turned the corner, and disappeared.

That was the first and last time I saw my future girlfriend, wife, and mother of my children. In fact, it was close to the last time that anyone saw her except on film. Jayne Mansfield died in a tragic car crash shortly after our chance meeting on Aspen Street.

She may have left me forever, but at least I had a photo to remember her by.

Stretched out on a sheet of glossy photo paper, Jayne Mansfield reclined on her back in all of her bountiful glory. She wore a black fishnet body stocking that hugged her hourglass figure from the tips of her toes and over her ample round breasts to the nape of her milky white neck. The stocking left little to the imagination.

She signed the photo, "To my darling Phil, all my love, Jayne."

I slipped the picture into my backpack and ran home as fast as my size-five penny loafers could carry me without combusting in flames. I couldn't wait to tell my mom about the amazing lady I met on my way home from school, about the big black limousine, about the proof I had tucked in my backpack for safekeeping inside the pages of my Catholic school bible.

I flung open the side door of our house and raced into the kitchen. "Momma! Momma!" Ya won't believe what happened! I met this lady, this lady, and I, I, I, I, I, well, ya just won't believe it, I, I, I..." She interjected, "Calm yawself down or yawl have an asthma attack."

I reached into my backpack, slipped Jayne Mansfield out of the bible, and excitedly handed the 8 x 10 glossy of near-nakedness to my mother. "Look!"

She almost fainted. "Oh, Philip! You shuh'nt be lookin' at a pitchah like this. It's so indecent!" Based on my doctor exam with Regina, I wondered if it was also immoral.

I watched in shock as Mom tore Jayne into tiny pieces and tossed her in the trash can.

When my older brother Ted arrived home from high school, I told him what had happened that afternoon. He divulged that he had staked out a spot across the street from the neighbor's house on numerous occasions, but Jayne never materialized.

We carried the trash can and a roll of scotch tape upstairs to his bedroom in the attic and laid out the pieces of Jayne on his desk.

But even my brother, the family puzzle master, couldn't put Jayne back together again.

7

THE VIRGIN BIRTHS

"Patience is a virgin."
- Archie Bunker

My mom and dad were understudies of the Pope and Mother Theresa, poster parents of the Holy Roman Catholic Church.

Dad was an avid practitioner of the adverb "religiously." He religiously attended 6:00 morning mass five days a week, slipped five-dollar bills into the collection plate, and oversaw church service organizations that collected everything from eyeglasses to canned soup for poor families (actually, "everything" except condoms, a form of birth control outlawed by envious celibate bishops who ran the church).

Our postman must have thought our house was the global headquarters of Third World Charities, Inc.

The names of the charities changed, but the pictures on the "Please Help" envelopes always looked the same: Babies with distended bellies, emaciated mothers carrying clay jugs of swamp water on their heads, African children with sad eyes holding empty wooden food bowls.

I always admired my parent's generosity and suspected that their framed photos were hung at the entrance to a Little Sisters of the Poor cinderblock schoolhouse in Zimbabwe.

The 40 days of Lent before Easter were rife with Catholic traditions in our house. On the first day of Lent, Ash Wednesday, Mom dragged the two-foot Virgin Mary statue out of the hall closet and placed her atop an antique walnut end table that served as a makeshift altar in the living room.

Every night after supper, for 40 consecutive nights, we paid homage to the Virgin. She looked over us with her Mona Lisa smile as we got down on our knees on the plush gold carpet and prayed the rosary*. This unique piece of Catholic jewelry featured a string of 59 beads ending in a cross and was used to count down a series of 59 prayers.

Each night, when we prayed, my bow-tied father selected one of us to lead the rosary. He chose us in equal rotation to spare me, my brothers, and my sister (who is named Mary and is not a virgin) the shame and embarrassment of being passed over, which would almost certainly inflict a sense of spiritual inadequacy.

My brother Richie and I discovered that it took about 45 minutes on our throbbing knees to complete a rosary prayer session.

* If you want to pick up a rosary for yourself, Google "rosaries," and you will find enough websites to keep you in prayer beads through eternal life. My personal favorite is on RosaryMart.com, which, second only to IndestructibleProstheticLeg.com, holds claim to the most specialized e-tail site on the worldwide web. For only $13.95, you can purchase the famed Swarovski Crystal "Cat Eye Papal Rosary." If you worship cats, this is your rosary. Caveat emptor: the beads are faux cat eyes, not real eyes extracted from Siamese kittens that once roamed the hallowed halls of the Vatican.

We theorized that this record could be beaten through intensive memorization and rosary rehearsal time. Thus began our secret game, known only to us as "The Speed Rosary." Richie and I showed up at rosary time armed with pocket watches hidden in our jeans. On your mark, get set, ready, pray. We simultaneously reached into our pockets and punched the start buttons on our watches.

Richie raced through the first bead, "HolyMaryMotherOf-GodBlessedAreYouAmongWomenAndBlessedIsTheFruitOf-ThyWombJesus.PrayForUsSinnersNowAndAtTheHourOfOur DeathAmen."

Sweat dripped down my temples as Richie continued his feverish pace through the first four of the five sets of beads. How could I ever beat his time? It had to be a rosary world speed record. Damn, he was good.

Barely able to distinguish the jumbled-together words of prayer, my father interjected, "Richie, slow down."

Ah hah! Now I had him. The last string of 10 beads cost Richie a full extra minute and a half. I could hear the anxiety in his "Glory Be to the Father...and to the Son...and to the Holy Ghost...Amen."

His final rosary time was 35 minutes, 28 seconds.

The secret to beating Richie was pacing. I experimented for hours to find the optimum speed that would help me to complete the rosary faster and with flawless diction.

I would not make the same mistake as Richie. My folks would be able to hear every word. I also worked on vocal tone. By lowering my voice to the soothing bottom end of the spectrum, I took the high-pitched edge off, creating the aural illusion of reverence.

The rehearsal hours paid off. When my night arrived to be the prayor, prayers to the Virgin Mary rolled off my tongue in immaculate succession.

I shaved 70 seconds off my brother's rosary record. Ultimately, though, Richie outsmarted me by deviously skipping several beads on the last night of Lent. No one caught on except me.

I knelt in silence as Richie lulled the rest of the family into a vegetative state with his new signature prayer voice, the monotone *"Speed Sleeper."*

The Virgin played mightily into our family beliefs, not to mention our sex lives.

Just as the Virgin never strutted her stuff, my parents took great care to remain fully clothed in front of us. When they kissed me goodnight, I assumed that they went to bed in the clothes they were wearing: my dad in his suit, bow tie, and wingtip shoes, my mom in her floral housedress and two-tone saddle shoes.

I imagined them lying on top of the shiny green satin bedspread, staring at the ceiling, all dressed up and ready to sleep.

The only thing separating us at night was a common wall between our bedrooms. Other than one episode of hearing Mom hysterically laughing, "Lou, stop!" I don't recall a single peep coming from their room that sounded like anything having to do with sex. Unwittingly, they spared me the repugnant mental image of parents, you know, doing it.

Until the age of 11, I firmly believed that my mom had a virgin birth—five times. That must have been why she called Bob, Ted, Richie, Mary, and me her little miracles.

In the late '50s and early '60s, stories of Virgin miracles popped up all over the world: a bleeding Blessed Mother statue in a town square in El Salvador, a picture of the Virgin Mary in a church in Madrid with tears rolling down her face, an apparition of the Virgin appearing in front of two blind girls in Guadalupe, Mexico (it made me wonder how they actually saw the Mother of God).

Even if we wanted to think about sex, the Virgin kept appearing in the newspaper to sweep our minds clean of impure thoughts. If that didn't work, our parents, the Pope and Mother Theresa, were always ready to serve as in-home substitutes for the Virgin.

This was never clearer to me than the day I walked home from Catholic school in the second grade. As I skipped up the driveway, I smelled smoke and heard the crackle of paper burning. I followed a cloud of gray smoke and floating embers to our small backyard.

My dad held a magazine open in a vertical position, which struck me as odd because magazines are read from left to right instead of from top to bottom. He thrust the magazine spread toward my mother's troubled face. "Dorothy, look at this filth!" My mother gasped and averted her eyes.

He tossed the magazine into the fire and repeated the process over and over. Well over 100 centerfold beauties burned that day, more than during the Salem Witch trials. It was the *Great Playboy Bonfire of 1960,* a towering inferno of naked photos from my older brothers' secret magazine stash.

By the size of the fire, I could tell that they were serious collectors. The entire soft-porn period of 1957 through 1960 went up in flames that afternoon.

I heard years later that my mother stumbled across the stack of *Playboy* magazines while vacuuming the bedroom my brothers shared in the attic. They created a clever removable face panel between the drawers on the front of their built-in wall-to-wall desk. One bump with mom's vacuum cleaner and the false panel crashed open, revealing the secret compartment of porn that could jettison my God-forsaken brothers into the fires of hell.

Our devout Catholic parents gave them an alternative to eternal damnation. My brothers went to confession, asked God for forgiveness, and promised never to buy *Playboy* again.

As it turned out, *Penthouse* was even better.

❧ 8 ❧

LADY LIBERTY GETS A HAIRCUT

"Gilligan, did you let the Skipper cut your hair?
It looks like he used a coconut shell as a bowl!"
- **The Professor**

E very Friday morning, on his way out the door, my dad plunked the week's allowance into my outstretched palm—a lonely, pitiful dime.

This was my reward for finishing chores. At seven years old and barely big enough to push a lawnmower, my chores included mowing the front and back lawns, weeding, washing our home's storm windows, snow shoveling, washing dishes after dinner, and carrying garbage cans out to the street on trash night.

My father's ulterior motive was simply to teach me how to manage a budget, a budget not unlike Ma and Pa Kettle's.

Rather than blowing my dime on a prank call from a phone booth, I invested in the original two-for-one offer: Bazooka bubble gum individually wrapped in five-panel Bazooka Joe comic strips. Not only did ten one-cent pieces last for days, but the cartoon speech bubbles showed my parents that I was becoming an avid reader.

That kind of responsible second-grader money management should have been enough to convince my father to bump my weekly allowance to a quarter dollar. The George Washington quarter was by no means a declaration of financial independence. But it provided enough extra purchasing power to buy, say, a ride on the coin-operated bucking bronco machine by the front doors of the A&P grocery store.

One "allowance Friday," I bypassed the dime, quarter, and half dollar and leaped directly to the coveted coin of every boy's and girl's dreams.

My father squeezed his oval rubber coin purse, plucked two gleaming silver dollars out of the slot, and plopped them into my hand.

I had just been given the Holy Grail of coins—1938 Lady Liberty Peace coins. A tiara of sunrays streamed from her noble head. Her side profile peered ahead to a future of peace and prosperity. A woman on the move is what she was, paving the way for freedom among all people, but mostly people in the U.S.A.

Illumined brilliance gleamed from the contours of her embossed face like shafts of sunlight sparkling across rolling Atlantic and Pacific swells. And, my God, what a back! Who could not be awed by her trusty eagle companion perched on a lofty peak, talons clutching an olive branch, ushering in the dawn of a new post-war age of international harmony?

All of these visions preoccupied my mind as I stared at Lady Liberty, transfixed by the magnitude of her beauty and value placed in the palm of my hand.

That is, I was transfixed until I wasn't when my dad said, "These are for your haircut. Bring me the change and keep a dime for yourself."

That afternoon, I faced the harsh reality that time was running out. I was expected to get a haircut while my dad was at work and my mom went shopping. I clutched the only silver dollars I would likely ever possess. Unless I came up with a fool-proof plan, my treasured coins would fall into the hands of the local barber.

I'd never given myself a haircut, but I figured, *How hard could it be?* After all, the barber was an old man with shaky hands. If he could snip my hair without puncturing my skull or clipping off an ear or eyebrow, so could I.

I hurried to the kitchen and grabbed a pair of scissors from the meticulously organized drawer where my mother stowed all the things needed for cutting, taping, mailing, and mending.

I realized my first problem when I could barely see myself in the high bathroom mirror above the sink. Even standing on my tiptoes, I wasn't tall enough to get a full view of my head. That didn't stop me from snipping away at the tufts of brown curls, starting with the right side of my head.

I accidentally chopped off a small chunk of my right ear and came close to giving myself a full Van Gough.

Not to be deterred, I snipped the hair on the east side of my head down to the scalp, leaving behind a mishmash of scissor cuts. My self-barber strategy had taken a sharp turn for the worst.

Thick waves of hair covered one side of my head. The other side was a barren, mutilated wasteland.

I saw trouble ahead. My mother would arrive home at any minute, greeted by her son, Young Phil Frankenstein.

I opened the medicine cabinet behind the mirror and proceeded to stick small band-aid strips on the wounds. My bandaged head resembled a patchwork quilt stitched together by Edward Scissorhands.

I had to dispose of the evidence. I collected my pile of hair from the sink, tossed it into a paper lunch bag, and dumped it into the garbage can in the backyard.

The only way out of my hair-brained mistake became obvious. I ran four blocks to the Floral Barbershop, one of only two barbershops in town. The other, Cappy's, was cheaper, but Cappy had built a reputation as the hair butcher of Floral Park.

As luck would have it, no other customers were in the barbershop. The hunchbacked owner, old man Rupert, took one look at my own butcher job and smirked, "What have we here, my boy? Looks like somebody tried to give himself a haircut, 'eh?"

Rupert must have been 80, if not older. Over the years, he'd probably come to the haircut rescue of dozens of blundering boys like me.

"Oh no, Mista Rupert, sir. I'll tell ya what happened. I just left Cappy's, and look! Please fix what he did to me, Mista Rupert."

To sweeten the deal, I reached into the pocket of my brown corduroy pants and held up the two silver dollars. "I'll even pay ya wit deese. They're 1938 Lady Liberty sillva dollahs, probably worth at least five hundred bucks!"

"Well, let's see what we can do, son," he replied with a grandfatherly grin. "A flattop should do the trick. And no one will be the wiser."

He lifted me into the big red leather and chrome barber chair and started up the electric razor. Mr. Rupert ran the blades in parallel rows across the west side of my head until it matched the bald-eagle east side. Then he mowed the back 40 down to the scalp. His trembling hands finished the job with a half-inch tall flattop. Mr. Rupert applied wax to the front of my shortly cropped hair, creating the appearance of a neatly trimmed garden shrub planted on my head.

Grateful and relieved, I thanked old man Rupert, handed

over both Lady Liberties, and in typical scatter-brained style, said, "Keep the change," forgetting that I was supposed to give the change to my father.

When I arrived home, my mother met me in the kitchen, stunned by my extreme no-hair haircut. "Philip! Look at yuh head! What happened to yuh?"

I threw my hands up in resignation and uttered the first word that popped into my head. "Cappy's."

❧ 9 ❧
ALL IN THE ECCENTRIC
FAMILY

*"Son, go in the kitchen and fix your
Aunt Esther a fish-head sandwich."*
- Fred Sanford

Visiting my grandparents' and aunts' house could be compared to, say, spending a Sunday afternoon at the carnival. While my Spanish grandfather and grandmother and first-generation American father spit on each other, lisping in Castillian, my Aunt Virginia's parrot, Fuji, joined in the conversation from his perch in the bird cage.

Grandpa: "Encén el meu cigar."

Fuji: "El cigar! El cigar! El cigar!"

My father did as the parrot asked in the mother tongue of Castillian Barcelona, "Light my cigar."

He reached into his gray pin-striped suitcoat pocket, flipped open the silver top of his butane lighter, and lit Grandpa's cigar, his cigar, and finally, Grandma's. The dark green hand-rolled Habaños, slightly smaller than police nightsticks, were shipped illegally to New York by Grandpa's "contacts" in Cuba.

My grandmother's wealthy father had owned a sugar plantation in Cuba. After my grandparents married and had their first six children, the family moved to Cuba to run the plantation.

In 1920, when Prohibition criminalized the sale of alcohol, my grandfather sipped rum, smoked cigars, and played violin 1500 miles away from the Feds on the porch of the plantation house.

While Grandpa fiddled and cane sugar prices plummeted, the plantation fell into ruin. His father-in-law banished them from the property. Overnight, they descended from riches to rags.

With eight mouths to feed and no prospects for work, the future looked bleak. Grandpa contacted his father, who owned a successful Spain-England import-export business originally based in the port city of Liverpool. My great-grandfather agreed to have Grandpa help him run the new, growing New York City branch of the business.

My grandparents soon faced another minor obstacle called the Great Depression. The business collapsed. Grandpa started and ended a series of new careers in which he had no experience—insurance salesman, newspaper editor, and whatever other jobs he could charm his way into without qualifications.

Grandma knit and sold ladies' beaded handbags. My father and his brothers worked to support the family while the daughters studied in school. All eight of them were packed into a rundown house in the new suburbs of Long Island.

Fast forward to the 1960s. Grandpa, Grandma, my middle-aged single aunts Eileen and Virginia, Fuji the parrot, and a glass tank of tropical fish lived together on the first floor of the multi-generational Caragol family home.

Grandpa slept in a single bed behind a curtain in the living room. Grandma slept in a single bed in the front parlor, comparable to catching 40 winks in an oversized egg carton. My aunts slept in twin beds in the converted dining room.

Aunt Marguerite lived on the second floor with Uncle Johnny, young cousins Michael and Peter, and their singing German Shepherd, Major. Going upstairs to visit them required entering a small bathroom on the first floor and exiting through a second door to access the stairwell. I remember opening the first door and surprising Grandpa, who sat on the toilet smoking a cigar. He yelled, "Felip! Sortir!" My father translated from the faded and cracked living room behind me. "Philip, get out!"

After Grandpa emerged from his privy sanctuary, I ventured upstairs. Major greeted me on the landing, waiting to perform his opening aria.

I voiced the command, "Sing, Mayjah, sing!" He raised his head toward the ceiling, called on the spirits of his wolf ancestors, and howled, "Wooooooooooooo. Wahooooooooooo! Rooo roooo roooo wahoooooooo!"

Major led me into the cramped, cluttered living room that Aunt Marguerite had converted into her pottery studio and showroom.

She sat at one of a half-dozen card tables, a lit cigarette with bright red lipstick marks dangling from her mouth. She painted the purplish tail feathers of a ceramic rooster using the fine bristles of an artist's brush. Roosters were her specialty, and they supplemented Uncle Johnny's income.

Her collectors bought roosters of all shapes, sizes, and descriptions—rooster ashtrays, rooster lamps, decorative tabletop roosters, front porch and garden roosters, character roosters that smoked cigars, cockfighting roosters sporting ruby-colored boxing gloves.

Roosters filled the room and created the impression of a ceramic barnyard. Gray clay roosters, perched on card tables, awaited their turn to be baked, painted, and glazed.

Standing rooster lamps lined one wall, all featuring light bulbs growing out of the crimson combs atop their heads.

Floor-to-ceiling shelves displayed a flock of rooster figurines, serving platters, coffee mugs, and salt and pepper shakers.

Uncle Johnny appeared in the doorway. Short and thin, without a visible ounce of fat on his frame, my uncle stayed in shape as a runner on the floor of the New York Stock Exchange.

I thought the brown bottle of beer in his hand was a permanent fixture because I never saw him without one.

During WWII, he served as a defense worker at the Grumman Aviation plant in Farmingdale, Long Island. He helped manufacture the iron hooks that aircraft carriers used to catch and brake Wildcat fighter planes landing on the deck.

The deafening roar of machinery in the plant took a toll on his hearing. "Hello" sounded like "HELLO!"

"HELLO! IS THAT MY FAVORITE NEPHEW? TO WHAT DO WE OWE THE PLEASURE OF YOUR VISIT, PHILIP?"

"My folks brought me ovva to see Grandma and Grandpa, so I thought I'd stop by as long as I'm he-ah."

"YOU WANT A BEER? A BOY AFTER MY OWN HEART BUT I DON'T THINK YOUR PARENTS WOULD LIKE THAT."

"No, I said *he-ah*, not *be-ah*."

"HA HA, OF COURSE YOU DID! FOLLOW ME TO THE KITCHEN. I GOT SOMETHIN' TO SHOW YOU."

The kitchen was small and typical of the period. Knotty pine cabinets created the cozy atmosphere of cooking in a cabin with Daniel Boone's frontier wife, chopping vegetables by the sink with a hatchet.

A pea-green refrigerator and matching electric stove added a futuristic flair as seen on TV in the kitchen of George and Jane Jetson.

A canary-yellow Formica table and four matching padded chrome chairs provided a stylish hub for exquisite family meals of spam loaf, instant mashed potatoes, and dessert bowls of lime green Jell-O with marshmallows.

Uncle Johnny said he'd be right back. I rolled my fingertips impatiently on the table and waited.

He returned with a scallop-edged black-and-white snapshot. For the first time, he spoke to me in a soft voice just above a whisper.

Uncle Johnny pointed to the man in the photo. "I wanted to show you my friend Marty. Michael and Peter call him Uncle Marty even though he's not a relation. This is a picture of him in his army outfit. He fought in the Pacific in World War II. You notice anything different about him?"

I scanned the picture. "Well, shaw. He reminds me of Blackbee-ahd the pirate, only without the bee-ahd, on account of his eye patch."

He laughed. "Good eye, Phil. You picked right up on it."

"How'd he lose his eye?"

Uncle Johnny choked up with emotion. He breathed in sadness and exhaled grief.

"Well, Phil, it's like this. Marty lost his eye in a battle of Iwo Jima."

"That's terrible, Uncle Johnny!"

"And I lost Marty this week after his battle with cancer."

Next thing I knew, Aunt Marguerite yelled something indistinguishable from her studio. We raced in. She screamed out of the raised second-story window, "Peter, you come down from that tree right now!"

I saw my cousin Peter high up in the elm tree in front of the house. He must have climbed 30 ft. above the sidewalk in sneakers. No hook-and-ladder firetrucks were called to get him down. No ropes were thrown to him. Peter was treated like most boys in the '60s—if you found your way into a jam, you had to find your own way out.

My other cousin, Michael, was more reserved, brainy, and

clever enough to never get caught. While Peter scampered down the tree limbs, Michael and I played checkers. Correction. Michael played, and I watched as he jumped over my checkers in zigzag patterns I failed to notice.

Three losses later, I said goodnight and headed downstairs. Grandma, Grandpa, and my dad hadn't budged an inch since I left them an hour earlier.

Unless my imagination got the better of me, I swore those cigars lasted longer than the Cuban revolution.

———

Grandpa died first. I'd never seen a dead person. Mourners approached his open casket at the Dalton funeral home to say goodbye. I overheard a conversation between two old ladies. They said the oddest things.

"He looks so natural, doesn't he, Blanche?"

"Yes, Bernice. And what a handsome suit."

"The white boutonniere is a nice touch."

"Are those cufflinks silver or platinum?"

"Silver. Definitely silver, Bernice. They match the tie clip."

"You're so right, Blanche. My Ralph has the same tie clip and it's definitely silver. Why spend all that money on platinum when it still looks like silver?"

To me, Grandpa looked anything but natural and more like a lesser-known figure from Madame Tussaud's Wax Museum. Death is a foreign concept to the young. It needs to be touched to be understood.

Between mourners, I cautiously walked up to Grandpa's casket. He was present in his body, but his spirit went missing. The spirit counts. It's not easy to define, but it seems to be the difference between being alive and being a lifeless form in a wax museum.

I mustered my courage and laid my hand on Grandpa's. His

hand felt cold, stiff, and unable to reciprocate with his usual affectionate squeeze.

I leaned down and whispered into his ear. "Sorry for that time I bahdged inta the bathroom, Grandpa. We di'nt spend much time togethah, but I'll miss our Sunday aftanoons. You're not he-ah, but I know way-ah you are. Say hi to Saint Peeta and have a cigah for me in heaven."

Six months later, Grandma died of heartbreak. Her death hit my father hard and deep. Their mother-son bond was strong.

The evening Grandma died, my brothers, sister, mom, and dad gathered around the dinner table. Mom prepared my father's favorite Spanish dish, *arroz con pollo*.

The cast iron skillet in the center of the table brimmed with tender roasted chicken thighs, Spanish rice, hunks of spicy chorizo, tender white beans, and the zesty aroma of rosemary sprigs and smoked paprika.

During the lean times when my father was a boy, Grandma reserved *arroz con pollo* for special birthday meals, the ingredients purchased with food ration stamps she had saved for the occasion.

Mom stood up from the table, dipped a ladle into the skillet, and filled the first bowl. She wanted the first bowl to be for my father, her husband, to comfort him in his grief.

When Mom set the bowl in front of Dad, memories of his mother came flooding back. He broke down and wept with the tears of a lost son.

None of us had ever seen Dad cry. We all cried with him. We cried for him. He was not the completely undefeatable and indefatigable man we thought he was.

We loved him. And in that ethereal moment, we glimpsed a deeper version of the father we had never fully known.

❧ 10 ❧

A SHARK TALE

"I think we're going to need a bigger boat."
- Matt Hooper, *Jaws*

W hen my maternal grandparents died, they weren't rich. But they were generous. They left $13,000 from their modest "estate" to my mom and dad, enough to build an affordable brown-shingled vacation home in the Hamptons and to buy a small aluminum boat, a vessel that plunged our family of sea rookies into battle with a creature from the deep.

Lesser-known Hampton Bays didn't hold the filthy rich allure of jet-setter South, West, and East Hampton. Almost no one in Hampton Bays owned beachfront mansions or 100-foot party yachts teeming with .0001-percent trust funders, starlets, or Wall Street moguls having wild sex on a mess table in the galley.

Hampton Bays attracted middle-class working families who more closely resembled cast members of *The Old Man and the Sea* than the fat cats in *The Great Gatsby*.

While high and mighty multi-millionaires plowed through

the bay in their luxury battleships, we struggled to plow through the surging waves left in their wake. The only way to avoid capsizing in our dinky 12-foot aluminum motorboat was to punch through the waves head-on.

My bare-chested father would yell, "Hold on, boys!" as he gunned the sputtering 10-horsepower Evinrude outboard engine from his skipper's bench at the stern of the boat.

Getting into risky situations on the water both thrilled my father and scared the hell out of Richie and me. Dad hung out his law office shingle in 1940 and committed himself to the humdrum practice of drawing up wills for almost every man and woman over the age of 50 within a 20-mile radius.

He knew a thing or two about death through client *rigor mortis*. He wasn't afraid to face the Grim Reaper on land or sea. It probably didn't occur to him that we might go down with him to Davy Jones's locker, our lives cut short, pinched to death by lobsters and crabs at the muddy bottom of the bay.

In September 1960, Hurricane Donna struck the Eastern seaboard. Sustained winds of 110 miles per hour slammed into the coast. The Hamptons took a direct hit. Towering walls of waves battered Dune Road in West Hampton. The half-mile-wide strip of dunes, dotted with stately vacation homes, was the only barrier between the Atlantic and Shinnecock Bay in Hampton Bays.

After the hurricane, with the winds subsiding but still howling, our thrill-seeking pop woke my brother and me before dawn with an unsettling invitation. "Rise and shine, boys! Get dressed! We're taking a ride to Dune Road!"

Richie and I threw on our sweaters, canvas jeans, and quilted plaid jackets and raced out to our car—the Rambler Ambassador, a five-passenger family muscle car featuring a

270-horsepower V-8 engine, squarish body, tail fins, and Flash-O-Matic transmission activated with chrome push button controls on the dashboard.

We could see that Dad was amped up, eager to be one of the first to experience an apocalyptic tour of Dune Road destruction. He led us out to the garage. Our high-strung pop was on a mission to get to Dune Road before the fire engines and police showed up around sunrise. "Come on, boys. Get in! Get in! Let's go before they close the road!" And, yes, based on his lack of impulse control, I'm pretty sure Dad also had undiagnosed ADHD.

He turned the ignition key, pushed in the "R" Flash-O-Matic button on the dash, and away we went, screeching in reverse out of the driveway. He pressed the "D" button and slammed the gas pedal to the floor. All 270 horses roared like a jet engine, propelling us at a new Hampton Bays land speed record toward Dune Road.

My father drove so fast that everything outside the car window became a passing blur. Several times, I heard "ka-clunks" under my feet and wondered if we might see a trail of flattened chipmunks, seagulls, and box turtles splattered across the narrow road when we drove home (hopefully, alive) on the return trip.

Richie and I held on for dear life in the back seat. I glanced into the rearview mirror. I'd never seen Dad with such a wild look in his eyes. He accelerated when we reached the final stretch over the Ponquogue drawbridge, only a half mile before Dune Road.

Flashing red lights and crossing gates at the peak of the arched bridge alerted our lone car that the drawbridge was about to separate and rise from the roadway to make way for a battered sailboat too tall to fit under the span.

Richie and I dove on the floor. Dad stepped on the gas pedal and launched the Ambassador, rocket style, up and over the drawbridge just before the gates dropped behind us and cut us off from civilization.

When the road ended, he wrenched the steering wheel in a hair-raising right turn. We fishtailed around a slick sandy corner and slid to a full stop in the middle of Dune Road. Our intrepid trio finally made it—Dad gripping the wheel of his thrill-seeking mid-life crisis, my nauseous brother and I holding down last night's meatloaf and mashed potatoes dinner. We were too young to die and years away from even having the chance to sprout pubic hair.

The car idled, trembled, and growled a deep rumble not unlike a heavy-breathing lion after the chase. We sat in stunned silence and stared out the panoramic windows of the Rambler.

Morning's first light formed a thin gray line between night and day above the eastern horizon. My brother's raised eyebrows formed worry lines that underscored two thoughts: *We could have died,* and *We still could* die.

The Rambler slowly rolled forward, carrying us into the post-storm Armageddon known to us as *Dune Road Meets Hurricane Donna.*

We spotted the first signs of destruction. The dunes between us and the raging ocean were mountainous, piled high with new sand deposited by the waves. Marshlands on the other side of the car stretched out into the bay, now suffocated under mounds of ocean seaweed. Shallow rivers of saltwater carved channels in the road between islands of sand-blasted pavement.

In a way, we felt robbed. The hurricane had ripped through the dunes with no signs of property destruction, *real* destruction like in *King Kong vs. Godzilla* when those bad boys laid waste to Manhattan.

We didn't drive far before the scattered remains of the first mansion came into view.

Up ahead, we saw what appeared to be a giant dollhouse tipped over on its side on top of the dunes.

The hurricane had knocked the sprawling four-story gray-shingled home off its foundation. The entire first floor was eerily intact, but the floors were ripped out, giving us a full view of the rooms inside.

The interior walls held together a striped wallpapered kitchen, grand teakwood paneled living room, two subway-tiled bathrooms, an empty five-car garage, and a dozen powder, play, reading, office, storage, and laundry rooms, all stripped of appliances and furniture. It looked like a life-size Matel playhouse where a giant Ken and Barbie once spent lazy summer afternoons sipping Long Island Iced Teas from glass tumblers the size of grain silos.

An endless string of palatial beach houses stretched far into the distance, all smashed to smithereens and strewn across the dunes.

Godzilla could not have done a better job of thrashing the beachfront vacation playground of the West Hampton rich and famous.

The waves that pounded West Hampton during Hurricane Donna also carved a new ocean inlet to the bay, wide and deep enough to float the Queen Mary.

The channel formed an aquatic expressway. Game fish never before seen by weekend boaters and swimmers teemed into the bay.

Man-sized tuna, striped bass, and sharks spread out in territorial positions to claim their share of the marine smorgasbord. They sucked up swarms of herring, minnows, blue snappers, fluke, flounder, eels, and blue claw crabs faster than an underwater shop vac.

The threat of "death by shark" hung in the air. Clam diggers who raked the bay in waist-high water ran to shore as great-finned creatures angled toward them, breaking the surface of the murky water. Beaches along the bay emptied of sun worshippers afraid they'd become shark lunch during otherwise refreshing breaststrokes. It was just a matter of time before water skiers started carrying spear guns and grenades as they scanned the water behind their power boats.

This in no way deterred our father, the bare-chested skipper, from puttering around the bay in our aluminum skiff, approximately the size of a Coast Guard stretcher.

Dad, Richie, and I always wore authentic captain's hats for boat rides. They were made of black canvas sporting an embroidered anchor on the front side and a curved black brim so small it provided no nose shade.

While lumbering along at five miles per hour with the motor opened to full throttle, Dad spotted a dorsal fin slicing through the water's surface. He turned the boat forty-five degrees and headed directly at the beast. Richie and I shifted to the center of our bench seats and held on. Neither of us wanted to be close to the sides of the boat where a shark might raise its head and chomp off our arms.

We sat with our backs to the bow and faced our father, whose teeth clenched the soggy stub of his cigar. He steered the motor with one hand and braced himself for battle with a tight grip on the handle of the bright orange gas tank next to his feet. Onward we went, closer and closer to the shark, appearing larger and larger the nearer we got.

When we approached the shark, my heart leaped in my chest. God help us. The shark was enormous, longer than the boat. We were no match for the monster from the deep.

Richie and I hoped that the excited wild man steering our puny fishing tub would come to his senses before it was too late. But hope was not enough to reverse the course of our father's quest for high-seas adventure.

On the bright side, he taught us a life-long lesson that day: In desperate situations, hope may not be enough to save you.

When we reached the shark, Dad yelled, "Richie, smack him with the paddle!" My young brain couldn't quite grasp our father's fearless command. A boy-eating shark paralleled the boat. Wouldn't smacking it with an oar make things worse? What if the shark attacked us and flipped the boat? Richie tugged on the oar with all his strength. Thankfully, the shark smacker was immovably pinned under the metal struts that secured the oar to the sidewall of the boat.

Some primal seafarer's alarm rang in the subconscious that was my dad's survival instinct. He swiftly changed course *after* he ran over the shark. As we passed over the shark's back, a bright red line appeared from tail to head, a battle wound inflicted by the outboard engine's whirling propeller.

I silently thanked the shark for not flipping the boat and eating us whole. I prayed that the wound didn't hurt too much and that he'd be ok. My dad doused his cigar stub in the bay, and we puttered home.

That night, we drove over to my Uncle Eddie's, Aunt Marion's, and cousins' cottage for a barbecue of charcoal-grilled hamburgers, hot dogs, potato salad, and corn on the cob.

Like most family gatherings, the evening began with happy hour. Uncle Eddie and Dad started the coals and stood around the grill, engaged in man talk. They sipped Cutty Sark scotch from glasses etched with the frosted image of a three-masted clipper ship.

I overheard Dad recounting the day's shark tale. "Eddie, I was a damn fool."

I took some comfort in my father's confession. He would never chase a shark again. Or so I hoped.

❧ II ❧
THE DAY THE MUSIC DIED

"From Dallas, Texas, the flash, apparently official. President Kennedy died at 1 p.m. Central Standard Time, 2 o'clock Eastern Standard Time."
- Walter Cronkite, CBS News, Nov. 22, 1963

A uthor's note: I hesitated to include this story about JFK's assassination in an otherwise lighthearted memoir. But no first-person account of growing up in the 1960s would be complete without a chapter describing how those three days in November 1963 affected us when we watched the historic tragedy unfold on our hazy black and white television screens.

2:10 p.m. EST, Friday, Nov. 22, 1963

Our old, stone-faced fifth-grade teacher, Mrs. Sampson, had just finished chalking a math lesson in long division on the blackboard when the announcement broke in through the pine speaker box mounted above the classroom door. The principal's voice cracked. Someone cried in the background.

"Teachers and students, may I have your attention, please? It is my sad duty to inform you about dreadful news that we have heard on the radio. Minutes ago, we learned that...that... our beloved President Kennedy was pronounced dead after being shot in his motorcade earlier today in Dallas, Texas.

"We are closing school early so you can go home to be with your families. May God bless Mrs. Kennedy, her children, the nation, and our community as we mourn the tragic loss of our president. Please take this time to honor President Kennedy by leaving the building in silence."

We had no choice but to leave our Catholic grammar school in silence. I peered around the room. My classmates were at a loss for words. We were in shock, adrift in a dream world where reality and impossibility vied for our attention. Mrs. Sampson asked us to gather our coats and books and to walk home safely.

As we exited the classroom, she slumped down in her desk chair, cupped her hands over her face, and sobbed. That was the moment when reality crept into our young bones. Our stern teacher rarely displayed emotion. If the announcement affected her so deeply, the news of JFK's assassination must have been true.

Like most kids in those years of post-war innocence, I felt a close connection to JFK. He was a personal and international sensation—the youngest president in U.S. history, movie-star handsome, a decorated war hero, and an inspiring orator. He came into our homes at the dawn of television for fireside chats, calming words of assurance from the Oval Office, charismatic speeches from Dublin and Berlin, and behind-the-scenes family getaways from the Kennedy compound on the summer shores of Cape Cod.

Even though JFK and I had never shaken hands or spoken

face-to-face, I thought of him more as an admired adult friend than a distant president leading the world's most powerful nation.

He taught us that, "Every accomplishment starts with the decision to try." And "try" he did.

JFK vowed we would land a man on the moon and bring him safely back to earth before the decade's end, a thrilling prospect to me and childhood fans of space-adventure TV shows like *Flash Gordon*, *The Twilight Zone*, and *Johnny Quest*.

He protected us from a Russian nuclear attack during the Cuban Missile Crisis, a hair-trigger event that could have obliterated the Eastern United States, where I lived with my family, friends, and neighbors.

He established the Peace Corps and embraced our younger generation as the new leaders of a better, more equal, more service-minded people.

I hurried home and found my mother, with mascara-streaked cheeks and a tear-soaked handkerchief clutched in her lap, intently focused on the black and white TV screen in our finished basement.

Soon, my father, sister, and brothers joined us. We watched the story unfold at the pace of a page-turner crime novel.

An ambulance left the Dallas hospital carrying the casket of JFK's lifeless body after a Catholic priest performed the Last Rights. My father leaned forward in his cushioned armchair as a reporter described the scene on the Dallas airport runway.

Jackie Kennedy stood by her husband's flag-draped casket in her blood-splattered skirt while Secret Service agents carried the president's body up a flight of stairs to the rear of Air Force One.

Another TV reporter described the swearing-in of our new 36th President, tall Texan Lyndon Baines Johnson, who took the oath of office inside the airplane's small, crowded conference room with a stoic Mrs. Kennedy and Ladybird Johnson by his side.

3 p.m. EST, Friday, Nov. 22, 1963

Within an hour, the mood in our family shifted from shock to anger. Dallas police in white-brimmed Stetson hats paraded the president's suspected killer in front of the press. A lightning storm of flickering camera flashbulbs erupted in the basement hallway of Dallas police headquarters as the TV station broadcast our first glimpse of Lee Harvey Oswald after his capture in a local movie theater.

Reporters shouted questions at the handcuffed prisoner as he was escorted down the hall. "Did you shoot the President?" Oswald answered with a matter-of-fact claim of innocence, "I haven't shot anybody. I haven't been told what I'm here for."

I screamed at the television. "Lie-ah! Lie-ah!"

12:21 p.m. EST, Sunday, Nov. 24, 1963

On Sunday morning, our family attended nine o'clock Mass. The church was packed with neighbors who came for comfort, to pray, to be together, and to share our grief in the aftermath of the assassination. When the black-robed priest led a prayer for the repose of the soul of JFK, weeping echoed off the stone walls of the sacred space. Husbands and wives clasped hands. Children hugged their parents to console them and to be consoled.

When Mass ended, the church emptied. A waterfall of mourners rushed home to watch the non-stop news coverage, a first for American television. So much had transpired in three days. The assassination. A new president. Oswald's arrest.

Hour by hour brought new information punctuated by stunning changes of events. Even at ten years old, I realized that

I was witnessing a tragedy unfold that would be written in history books. The mirthful music of our post-war life had been laid to rest in a violent crescendo. Almost overnight, our safe, wide-eyed, idyllic world had marched away into a shadowy cave of pessimism, fear, and despair.

When my mother unlocked the side door of our house, we piled into the basement and turned on the TV. At noon, Mom brought a tray of sliced bread, ham, cheese, mayonnaise, dill pickles, and homemade potato salad from the kitchen.

We were making sandwiches when I heard the "crack! crack!" and looked up at the screen. A man in a dark suit and gray fedora fired a pistol at Lee Harvey Oswald at close range after he exited an elevator in the basement of Dallas Police headquarters to be transferred to jail. Oswald doubled over. His mouth gaped open in a silent scream. His eyes clamped shut in agony.

Along with millions of other families watching the broadcast, we were ordinary middle-class Americans and first-hand witnesses to an extraordinary turn of events. We watched, in disbelief and in real-time, what we'd never seen before—a point-blank execution on live television.

Some praised Mafia-linked nightclub owner Jack Ruby for discharging justice on JFK's killer. Others despised Ruby for killing Oswald before all of the evidence could have been exposed in a murder trial.

As for me and other naïve young boys, I barely understood the concept of justice. I only knew that I had just seen a man shot dead while watching television with my family after church on a Sunday afternoon in November. And that memory has never faded into the shadows, no matter how hard I've tried to erase it.

2:17 p.m. EST, Sunday, Nov. 24, 1963

Presidential tragedy melted into somber pageantry. Two hours after Jack Ruby shot Lee Harvey Oswald, I watched the adored Mrs. Kennedy kneel at her husband's casket in the rotunda of the U.S. Capitol building. Her two young children, Caroline and John Jr., knelt beside her. I wished I could have been there. This was when the miracle of live television fell short; faraway footage disconnected us from the in-person community of mourners.

Two hundred and fifty thousand distraught Americans walked, drove, flew, or railed to the Capitol to pay homage to the president. A line of mourners stretched for three miles outside the rotunda.

They were old, young, conservatives, liberals, black, white, rich, homeless, educated, illiterate, lifelong citizens and newly arrived immigrants. Each paused at JFK's casket to pay their respects silently or aloud. Many wiped their eyes as they said goodbye to the great man they loved and admired.

It dawned on me, years later, that perhaps I had witnessed the ultimate justice. In his final act, JFK had temporarily broken down the barriers that separated strangers. Throngs of pilgrims from all walks of life, pilgrims who feared or distrusted each other, laid down their swords that day. They moved beyond prejudice to a momentary common ground of shared grief and empathy.

The TV camera zoomed in on a black grandmother from Tennessee. After standing in line for hours, she fainted and collapsed on the marble floor of the rotunda, dressed up in her Sunday-best coat and matching pillbox hat, popularized by the stylish Jacqueline Kennedy.

A distinguished-looking French diplomat in an expensive, knee-length woolen topcoat gave the woman a cup of water from his pocket flask and carried her through the line to the casket.

His act of benevolence was not lost on our father. "I hope

the world is watching. That's what it means to be honorable. That man did what JFK would have asked all of us to do."

Silence.

We watched the horse-drawn funeral caisson carry JFK's flag-draped coffin down Pennsylvania Avenue, lined with hundreds of thousands of the bereaved.

We all watched together when little John Jr. let go of his mother's hand, stepped forward, and saluted his father. And in that moment, we all broke down and held each other close.

A nation of tears carried John F. Kennedy to his final resting place in Arlington Cemetery, where an Eternal Flame still reminds us to never let the music die.

❧ 12 ❧

THE TIME BOMBERS

"Why do boys play with fire?
Because you can't build a space rocket with ice cubes."
- Paul Lynde

W e'll never know who started the first fire. Let's just say he was a bored Neanderthal cave kid named Zorg who rubbed a couple of flint stones together that shot a spark into a pile of dry grass and Woolly Mammoth bones. Little did Zorg know what he had started. Ever since, millions of boys have relished playing with fire, including my brother Richie and me, the night we fire-bombed the Carbinos.

Fire is merely a stepping stone to bigger boyhood pyrotechnic thrills. Fire leads to fire rockets. Fire rockets lead to firecrackers. And if you're really lucky, firecrackers lead to the bomb. The cherry red, thumb-sized M-80. According to urban legend, an M-80 contained the blasting power of a quarter stick of dynamite. It was exactly what my brother and I needed to scare the bejesus out of our cranky old neighbor, Mr. Carbino.

The Carbinos built their new home on a wooded lot three doors down from our brown-shingled summer cottage. They had moved from a brownstone in taxi-honking Brooklyn to retire in the solitude of our quiet lane in the seaside community of Hampton Bays, Long Island.

Their home builder also lived on the lane. Mr. Rafford of Rafford Construction was a kind, grandfatherly man. His weathered, sunbaked face always offered a ready smile. His sons were grown, married, and had moved away long before we arrived on Ludlow Lane. He took a shine to my brother and me. We were surrogate sons of sorts who brought a bit of youthful energy back into his life.

Mr. Rafford's generosity knew no limits, especially when it came to giving us construction materials for our boyhood projects. When we decided to build a clubhouse in our backyard, he donated cement cinderblocks for the foundation, leftovers from the construction of the Carbino's new house.

The three of us walked down the lane to the Carbino's side yard. The old couple were due to move in the next weekend. Mr. Rafford pointed out nine columns of cement blocks stacked up like a miniature Manhattan skyline. "They're all yours boys. You're doing me a favor by moving them off the property."

Richie and I were itching to start building. We ran home and returned with our Radio Flyer red wagon, a poor substitute for a flatbed truck but an easier mode of transportation than carrying the blocks by hand.

Each cinderblock weighed 40 lbs., about half of our individual body weights. Lifting blocks off the stacks and into the wagon was a heavy two-boy job. The wagon sagged under the weight of just two cement blocks. My brother pulled the wagon's long black handle, and I pushed on each exhausting trip up our bumpy gravel street. Beads of sweat trickled down our beet-red faces and soaked our *Leave It to Beaver*-style striped T-shirts.

When we finally reached our house, the wagon bumped up against sprawling tentacles of burly tree roots poking out of the lawn. The wagon toppled over when we tried to roll it over a fat, gnarled root. The blocks tumbled out onto Richie's foot. He limped across the yard with the wagon in tow.

In our backyard, a scraggly brier of thorn bushes surrounded the patch of open ground we picked for the building site. The massive bramble was both an obstacle and an integral part of our plan. It would form our clubhouse castle wall and thwart approaching intruders from entering our private keep, including, but not limited to our parents and the local horde of raccoons and skunks.

We snatched our dad's ax and new industrial-sized hedge clippers from the garage. We only needed to carve out a section of bushes wide enough to roll the wagon through.

Richie thrust the clippers into the bush and attempted to sever a main branch. "Argh! Damn! Crap! Son of a bitch!" he cried. The jagged thorns scraped his hands and arms, now bloody and stuck in the bush's stickery grasp.

I rushed to the garage and fetched heavy garden gloves and a second pair of rusty old clippers to cut Richie free from the boy-eating bush. But the stubborn bush was not going to willingly release its grip. The nasty thicket's spiked teeth bore down even harder on Richie's arms every time I jostled a branch with the clippers.

Next, I tried the ax, theorizing that chopping the limbs off at their source would allow Richie to back out with the section of bush attached to his arms for easier removal. I swung the ax over my head. The blade came down and hit its mark. A dozen more swings—and bingo! Richie stepped backward out of the bush, holding the dismembered tangle in his arms like a dance partner from shrubbery hell.

The ax left a perfect wagon gap in the sticker bushes. Richie's blood, sweat, and tears had opened a portal to the future home of our backyard lair.

Richie and I repeated the Radio Flyer journey over five

more grueling days. We loaded block upon block into the wagon, up the street, over the massive tree roots, through the thorn bushes, and stacked them for construction of the foundation.

On the last day, only two blocks remained. They rested one on top of the other in the dirt next to the Carbino's new drive-way. Finally, the backbreaking work would be finished.

We transferred the last two cinderblocks into the wagon and began the final trip to our backyard. The Radio Flyer's overworked, wobbly wheels squealed and clanked over the gravel stones. The blocks rattled, knocking against each other with the rising and falling motion of the wagon.

Mr. Carbino heard the racket and homed in on us. He had arrived earlier that Saturday. Movers had already unloaded the truck and carried all of the furniture, dishes, keepsakes, clothing racks, and appliances into the house.

The tired old man was in a nasty mood when he opened the front door and yelled, "Hey, you two! Where do you think you're going with my cinderblocks?"

Richie and I continued up the street. We naively hoped that our new neighbor would ignore us and not make a big deal out of our underage heist. "Stop right there, you hoodlums! Don't you hear me? Put those blocks back. Every one of them. Now! Or I'll call the police and have you juvenile delinquents arrested for robbery!"

The thought of lifting and dragging all those blocks back from our clubhouse was unthinkable. I answered him with what I considered to be a convincing counter-argument. "Mr. Rafford said we could have 'em. The blocks wuh leftovahs. We're buildin' a clubhouse and need deese for the foundation. Thank you. Yaw very generous!"

Mr. Carbino's response was unsympathetic. "I don't give a good goddamn what Rafford told you. I bought those blocks.

They're MINE, not YOURS. Bring them back, or you'll regret it —in juvey jail!"

"Jail" got our attention. Our father was a small-town lawyer and judge and had an upstanding reputation to protect. He wouldn't look kindly on front-page news that his sons were convicted of looting and sentenced to hard labor moving cinderblocks across the yard at a high-security penitentiary.

Beaten down and shoulders slumped, my defeated brother and I turned the wagon around. We unloaded the blocks under the watchful eyes of Carbino the Curmudgeon and returned over the next three days with wagon load after load, dumping each one haphazardly. No neat stacks. No skyline. Just a bunch of scattered cinderblocks for old man Carbino to sort out.

Richie and I decided then and there that Carbino would regret his demand. It was just a matter of plotting and time before we got even, just like we foiled Filbert, the corpulent camp counselor.

My brother's best friend, Kevin Chan, was well-connected to the underbelly of New York's Chinatown. Bootleg film reels? No problem. Cartons of cigarettes? Easy. Banned fireworks and explosives? Just ask.

Through Kevin's black-market connections, we procured a shoebox of M-80s. A plan went into motion that would shake Mr. Carbino's world and his house.

On a scorching August night, just after sunset, the Carbinos sat in their living room watching TV. They left their front door open for air circulation. Only a screen door separated them from my brother and me.

We snuck up to the porch and placed an M-80 under the door. To create a slow-burning fuse, Richie borrowed and lit one of our mother's long *Kent* menthol 100 cigarettes and inserted the M-80's waxy red fuse into the filter. The M-80 wouldn't explode until the cigarette burned down, giving us time to run home and have an airtight alibi when the explosion went off.

By the time the M-80 detonated, Richie and I had been on the couch with our dad, watching *The Wild Wild West* on TV for at least five minutes.

Minutes after the blast, Carbino came to our house and furiously rang the doorbell. Ding! Ding! Ding! Ding! Ding!

Our father sprang to his feet and marched to the door to find out what the ruckus was all about. Carbino shook his fist in our father's face. "Where are your sons?! The little hooligans just exploded a bomb on my porch! My wife almost had a heart attack!"

Dad returned the accusation with gusto. "What are you talking about? Don't you dare accuse my sons of that! They've been watching TV with me all night! Go home and cool off!"

He slammed the door in Carbino's face.

The Time Bombers evened the score thanks to luck, fatherly intervention, and the ancient boyhood tradition of playing with fire.

13

THE BREAKFAST HOST

"The Lord might be smilin' on the sheeps,
but they still wind up as lamb chops."
- Archie Bunker

I was raised near Archie Bunker's Queens neighborhood, where Catholics outnumbered trees and flowers. In 1908, our city fathers had a savvy sense of humor and marketing. They named our originally flowerless and treeless town *Floral Park*, the hometown where I was cut down to size one early November morning in an ill-fated altar boy breakfast feeding frenzy.

The city founder's marketing scheme worked. Flowers and trees were planted. By the 1920s, Floral Park was in full bloom. Waves of working-class Italians, Irish, Czechs, Germans, and Poles fled The City for a new life. They were as different as meatballs and corn beef. Yet, they shared the dream of suburban paradise and a belief in Catholicism, their one true faith that came with a V.I.P. pass up the stairway to heaven.

My mother and father were among them. In the extreme. A colossal collection of religious icons adorned our brick and stucco home, from various sizes of plastic and porcelain Virgin Mary statues to rosary prayer beads casually laid on the toilet tank as if to say, *As long as you're purging, why not pray and purge yourself of other blockages between you and the Creator?*

My parents enrolled me in our neighborhood Catholic school. Our teaching order of Saint Josephite nuns enlightened us that Catholic school would make us winners in God's eyes. It's probably why they named the school *Our Lady of Victory.* The name itself declared us victorious hobbit-sized warriors in the battle against worldly evil.

No boy escaped the job of altar boy in the adjoining brown-stone, stained-glass church. It resembled a mini Notre Dame cathedral, complete with the pungent ginger and charcoal scent of incense hanging in the air. So many Catholics attended our church that the priests added more and more Mass times to keep up with demand.

Want to watch football on Sunday morning? May we suggest the 5:00 or 6:30 p.m. Saturday Mass. Like to sleep in on God's day of rest? Choose the 9, 10:15 or 11:30 a.m. Sunday Mass.

The multitude of Masses required an army of altar boy recruits, ranging from the ages of eight to 13. We learned to speak Latin—which few of us understood. To a 10-year-old, *Ad altare dei* (at the altar of God) might have just as well meant, *Look! Something ad altare is stuck to the bottom of your shoe!*

The most dreaded altar boy assignment was the 6 a.m. weekday Mass. For five consecutive November days, I walked to church, shivering in the bone-chilling inky dark before sunrise.

One morning, my red-haired seventh-grade schoolmate Bernie and I dressed in our floor-length black robes and waist-length white linen blouse surplices. We were ready to go for the early Mass and waited for the priest in the Sacristy, the dressing room next to the altar where we would exit together to start the Mass.

Bernie and I were starving. Our stomachs groaned like the sound of Satan himself pulling apart the church rafters. In desperation, I pulled open the closed cupboard that held a large 50-gallon clear plastic sack of communion "hosts." The thin circular wafers were our only shot at a quick breakfast.

We shoved our hands into the sack and stuffed palms full of the hosts of the body of Christ into our famished mouths. The wafers miraculously congealed into swollen balls of Catholic cardboard.

When Father Keegan entered the Sacristy, our cheeks bulged like ravenous chipmunks. His startled eyes shifted from us to the violated sack of hosts. He seared into us, wild-eyed and red-faced. Bernie and I both accepted our fate. We were going straight to Hades.

"What've ya done, boys?" the Father demanded in his Irish brogue. The doughy mound of Godly hosts in our mouths rendered us nearly speechless. I could only manage to muffle, "Wee fowee fahfer. Pweeze fogiff uff."

From that day on, I never skipped breakfast before the early Mass. Not only did my soul depend upon never again consuming hands full of communion wafers, but Fruit Loops floating in a bowl of fresh cold milk tasted like a slice of heaven compared to the unsweetened body of the Savior.

According to Catholic teachings, communion wafers could be transformed into the actual body of Christ only when a priest "consecrated" them during the Mass, kind of like casting a secret spell at a Catholic magic show.

Once that happened, the wafers became the "hosts" of Christ's body. They had to be handled carefully and touched only by the approved holy hands of an ordained priest. Dropping a consecrated host was considered an atrocious act on par with body-slamming Jesus on the floor. I witnessed such a body slam at a Sunday Mass packed with horrified churchgoers.

Richie and I both served as altar boys that Sunday. We had recently completed altar boy training under the tutelage of the assistant priest, young Father Kevin.

He showed us how to light and snuff out the forest fire of tall candles standing on the main and side altars. We memorized every prayer we were expected to repeat during the Mass —in Latin, a foreign language about as useful to us as Swahili. We had no idea what we were praying for, which kind of defeated the whole purpose of praying.

To complicate matters, Richie and I had to remember when to stand, sit and kneel. I often stood when the rest of the church knelt, knelt when they sat, and sat when they stood up in the pews. I constantly corrected myself when I saw what the congregation was doing, popping up and down like a surprised Jack-in-the-Altar-Boy-Box.

We were also directed to ring a handbell at three specific points in the Mass when the priest held his hands over the golden chalice that contained Christ's consecrated blood, formerly cheap red table wine. We knelt facing the back of the priest, making it nearly impossible to see when his hands hovered over the cup.

Not wanting to miss his cue, Richie rang the bell whenever the priest's hands came anywhere near the chalice. At our first Mass, he rang the bell sixteen times. Afterward, silver-haired Father Alberto asked, "So, which one of you boys is the Swiss bell ringer?"

Our most important job happened alongside the priest at the communion rail. While he placed hosts on the tongues of worshippers who knelt at the rail, we held a "paten" under their chins. The golden paten bore a striking resemblance to its sporty cousin, the ping-pong paddle. We had to stay alert and always be prepared to wield the paten and catch the host if it accidentally slipped out of the priest's fingers or off the tip of a church member's tongue.

Richie and I had a clear view of each other as we worked the communion rail toward each other, accompanied by priests. I saw the whole catastrophe unfold in slow motion.

Richie's priest flung hosts into parishioners' mouths as if he were tossing Frisbees through the center of a tire target. A host left his fingers and clipped an old woman in the upper lip. Heads turned as the host flipped end-over-end in midair and began its descent toward the floor.

Richie jumped into action and scooped his paten under the host. He caught it, but his speedy scooping motion sent the host flying over the priest's head. Without a second to spare, Richie dove for the host. And down fell the body of Christ. Everyone watched as their beloved Savior plunged to the cold marble floor and smashed into pieces, just inches from Richie's outstretched hand.

The congregation gasped. Time stopped. As did the Mass. The priests asked the congregation to be seated while they executed the sacred protocol for resurrecting body-slammed Jesus from the floor. Five hundred of the faithful were riveted as they watched the priests bless and anoint a linen cloth with holy oil.

The priests knelt beside Jesus, wrapped him in cloth, and carried him to the tabernacle, a small tomb on the back altar where uneaten hosts were laid to rest.

It was not a good day for worshippers, particularly for Richie, who went down in defeat at Our Lady of Victory at the hands of a Frisbee-flinging man of God.

᪲ 14 ᪲
AND THEN THERE
WERE NUNS

"And there you heard a modern spiritual by Dale and Gail,
'One Toke Over the Line, Sweet Jesus.'"
- Lawrence Welk

W hat's black and white and red all over? A nun
falling down the stairs. That's the level of sick
humor that defined many of my Catholic
schoolboy friends in the 1960s. We were altar boys, street patrol
guards, and wisecrackers ruled by a waddle of penguins
married to Jesus.

Our teachers at Our Lady of Victory (OLV) were The Sisters
of Saint Joseph. The Josephites looked like Empress Penguins
in human form, from their black veil and pleated full-body
dress (named the "habit," I assume, because they wore one
every day) to the white headpiece, neck wrap, and chest bib
hiding their forbidden bosoms.

Their personalities ranged from sweet to terrifying. The
latter group was given secret nicknames—Sister Boniface,
affectionately called Sister Bony Face; Sister Saint Vincent,
renamed Vinny; and Sister Ann Maura, known simply as SAM.

Sister Bony Face was a poor choice for a teacher of innocent second-graders. A Catholic cauldron of pent-up fury, she could have made an anger management therapist throw a tantrum or been a champion water-boarder for the CIA.

When buck-toothed Tommy Edgars wrote with his left hand, she cracked his knuckles with a wooden ruler. When he attempted to write with his right hand, she marked his homework with a big red F and helpful feedback like "Unacceptable! You must try harder, or you will amount to nothing!"

The second time she caught Tommy writing with his left hand, she stormed over to his desk and pulled him by the ear to the front of the classroom. "Drop your pants and lay on my desk!"

All of us watched in horror as Sister Bony Face swatted the back of Tommy's legs with a yardstick. He screamed. Red welts spread across the back of his thighs.

That was the last day we saw Sister Bony Face, which made Tommy—and most of us—believe in miracles.

One steel-gray morning on my stroll to school, I spotted a furry lump in the middle of the sidewalk and knelt for a closer look. Black leathery wings. Pointy ears. Beady rat eyes. Vicious fangs and protruding pink tongue.

I had stumbled upon a dead bat, a creature of the night rarely seen by us city dwellers except in nature museums, books, or Count Dracula movies.

What a hideous sight and once-in-a-lifetime opportunity.

I ran home and grabbed an empty shoebox from my closet. Luckily, the bat was still on the sidewalk when I returned. I needed to lift the infectious little devil into the box without getting Rabies or, worse yet, transforming into a bloodsucking vampire. Every boy my age knew that bat bites were a sure way to join the ranks of The Undead.

I leaned over the flying rat. My long blue tie, monogrammed with OLV school letters, hung suspended over the tiny creature. I used the tie as a makeshift glove to pick up the bat and drop it into the shoebox. The bat landed on its back, staring straight up at me from its hideous fanged face.

The schoolyard soon became a Catholic horrorscape. I approached Kathleen Ryan, a curly-haired fifth grader decked out in her blue plaid school skirt, matching vest, starched white blouse, and blue beanie. "Kathleen, would ya like to see what I found on the way to school today?" I held the shoebox close to her intrigued face. "Are ya ready?" She nodded, wide-eyed, and eagerly awaited the mysterious surprise inside the box. I popped off the lid. She screamed and dashed away like the bat out of hell in the box.

The same scenario played out as I moved from girl to girl around the schoolyard. Open lid. Scream. Repeat. In retrospect, I confess I acted like a complete jerk. Sister Joey, the yard monitor, told me as much when she caught me scaring my sixth victim, little Ginny Alban.

I stayed after school that day in the detention room. Sister Joey ordered me to practice my penmanship on the chalkboard:

I will never scare girls again.
I will never scare girls again.
I will never scare girls again.
I will never scare girls again.
I will never scare girls again.

In my eighth year at OLV, the call went out for boys to volunteer as patrol guards. The job entailed standing at a crosswalk before and after school, stopping cars so students wouldn't get mowed down while crossing the street.

The nun who headed up the patrol guards, Sister SAM, hand-picked a dozen of us to attend a private recruitment session in the dim wood-paneled parlor of the convent. She tempted us to enlist by handing out the dashing white sashes we'd wear, adorned with an official Patrol Guard silver badge. "Go ahead, boys. Try them on."

We stood in a circle, our sashed chests puffed out in pride. In hopes of sealing the deal, SAM told us, "You will be elite men of the school, honored by your fellow students, the faculty, and God himself for your unselfish service."

She went on to inform us, "Just give it a try. Be a patrol guard for one week. If you don't like it, you can quit."

With nothing to lose, we all agreed to join. We would be school heroes with a guaranteed exit clause, looked up to by our peers and admired by The Creator. That said, it only took one day to realize that being a patrol guard was one of the most boring jobs in the world, on par with applying glue to envelope flaps on an assembly line.

I stood on a remote corner alone while other kids played in the schoolyard. During my first day on patrol, the skies opened. Sheets of icy rain drenched me like a frozen baboon on the deck of Noah's ark.

Worse yet, almost no cars drove on the side street where I was stationed, eliminating the thrill of saving school kids from meeting their maker at the front bumper of a speeding vehicle driven by some mom rushing to drop off her kid before the school bell rang.

At the end of the week, I approached SAM on the front steps of the school as she kept a watchful eye on the last students crossing the street on their way home. "Sista, I decided that the Patrol Gawds are not for me. Ya said we could quit if we din't like it. I gave it a shot. I wanna quit."

Her response has been seared into my brain ever since.

Even though I didn't want to hear it, I now appreciate the tough words of wisdom she taught me that day. "Mister Caragol, once a quitter, always a quitter."

I stayed on the Patrol Guards for the rest of the year. As a 71-year-old man, I still can't seem to quit anything I start without hearing SAM come back from the dead to haunt me.

Nuns were a common thread woven through the fabric of my youth. Even my older sister became an Empress Penguin. At the age of 18, right after graduating from high school, she joined a nursing order of nuns known as The Carmelites for The Aged and Infirm. We dropped her off at a convent in New York City, where my sister Mary became Sister Mary.

Her Mother Superior authorized paid tuition for Mary to attend nursing school. She spent the next three years earning her RN degree and caring for elderly residents at a bucolic nursing home nestled in the hills of Connecticut, owned and staffed by the good Carmelite sisters.

In the summer of 1967, Mary received a vacation slip and came home for a one-week visit. She was the fun, kind, sweet nun I had wished for in grade school. She wore her veil and habit well, a natural, loveable nun if there ever was one.

Our week together was filled with laughs, quiet evening conversations, big meals around the back porch picnic table, and several outings, including a night gone wrong at the local roller rink.

Sister Mary attracted the crowd's attention. At the rental counter, an older man paid for her skates. The rink's organist played a jazzy version of "Ave Maria." A couple skated up to her backward, "Hello, Sister. Welcome to the rink. Your outfit is far out!"

There were five in our group, including me, Richie, cousins Cathy and Barbara, and Mary. We held hands and formed a human chain, Mary and I being the last two links at the back.

We skated down the stretch together at full speed toward the bend at the end of the rink. When we rounded the corner, Mary picked up speed.

Our chain created a whip effect. Mary's hand slipped out of mine; her veil outstretched in mid-air behind her as straight as an ironing board. She was the original *Flying Nun* before Sally Fields landed the TV role.

Unable to slow down, Sister Mary plowed into the wall.

She survived without a scratch, a bride of Jesus robed in black and white. But, miraculously, not red all over.

❧ II ☙
THE PUBERTY YEARS
1965 - 1971 A.D.H.D.

*Holly, Richie and me before the BarcaLounger
Apocalypse.*

15

MY BRIEF LIFE OF CRIME

"Ah, the old bulletproof cummerbund in the tuxedo trick!"
– Maxwell Smart

Lots of the news stories I've read about a killer, kidnapper, or burglar contain this or a similar quote from a neighbor, "I'm shocked. He seemed like such a nice man." I wonder if it's also a shock to the man who committed the crime. "Hey. I'm a nice guy. I made a stupid mistake. I don't know what I was thinking when I filled that rental truck with two tons of explosive cow feces. I'm sorry. I'll never do it again. Promise!" I issued a similar confession (except for the cow feces part) after my capture as a pimple-faced teenage thief.

I never committed any serious crimes, but my brief period of teenage vandalism and shoplifting taught me that you don't have to be a psycho slinging a buzzsaw to be a law-breaking citizen. It can happen to a good person who makes a stupid mistake, too.

The inspiration for my brief life of crime came from Thomas Hewitt Edward Cat, the main character of the 1966 TV show, *T.H.E. Cat*. Thomas was a cat burglar Robin Hood, who stole from the rich and anonymously gave to the poor through his charitable foundations. As far as feline burglars go, he was the down-and-out's cat's meow.

Every Friday night at 8:00, T.H.E. slipped on his black ski mask, gloves and body suit, sprang across rooftops, and scaled walls with the grace and agility of a Bombay housecat. No wall safe hidden behind a fox-hunt painting stayed sealed for long when T.H.E. Cat placed his stethoscope on a safe door and slowly turned the tumbler clockwise and counterclockwise, culminating in a satisfying opening click.

Richie and I watched the show more as students in Cat Burglar 101 than as a couple of tweenagers taking in a night of TV.

We studied his moves. Never stand in the light. Stick to the shadows. Never step on a twig. Security guards are specially trained in the art of twig-snap listening, which foiled many a mansion heist. Never attempt to outrun a pack of Dobermans. Always befriend them with a juicy slab of beef generously sprinkled with a powder of pulverized sleeping pills.

Halfway through the fall TV semester, we Caragol brothers graduated to T.H.E. Cat Brothers. First, we had to find the perfect excuse that would convince our parents to let us go out after dark. Richie and I asked if we could walk to church to say our prayers before bedtime—a clever tactic only T.H.E. himself could have dreamed up during his youth.

Our parents not only permitted us, but they encouraged us to leave immediately so we'd have plenty of time to pray for our sins (which now included lying to our parents and possible cat burglary). Oddly, they never asked why their two sons were headed to church in black ski masks with matching coats, pants, and gloves.

That first night, my brother and I agreed to ease into our new criminal careers. We had no intention of stealing. Prowling the backyards of our neighbors would provide enough excitement for our test run as professional prowlers.

For a full hour, we slithered up driveways on our bellies, hopped over fences, leaped like cougars between backyard lawn shadows, crouched behind leafless bushes to avoid being seen (rookie mistake), and communicated through a series of secret hand signals pre-arranged by my cat burglar brother.

With our backs against the wall under the Kaminsky's lighted kitchen window, Richie pointed to a porcelain gnome standing in the center of the backyard on a small mound of dirt. Moonlight illuminated the shiny red-capped dwarf, giving the appearance of Sneezy, Bashful, or Doc in the spotlight about to break into a backyard rendition of "Whistle While You Work."

I could see the wheels turn in my brother's head. Prowling wasn't enough excitement. He stepped over to the dark side and aimed to kidnap Sneezy.

I snapped my head from side to side, a secret signal so secret that it didn't exist in our secret codebook: *No way I'm going out there where the Kaminskys can see us, catch us stealing Sneezy, call the cops, and have us arrested when we conned Mom and Dad into believing we're in church praying!* Then I pointed to my right temple and twirled my index finger in circles, the secret signal for, *You're crazy! Don't do it!* Next thing I knew, Richie sprang from the safe shadows of the Kaminsky's house out to the *Look, I'm a cat burglar!* moonlight beam on the lawn —cradling stolen Sneezy in his arms.

I instantly noticed our major wardrobe flaw. My brother's bright white Converse sneakers flickered like strobe lights as he ran across the lawn. He was a burglar mime, dressed in black and highlighted by white footwear for dramatic emphasis. I jumped up and down, wildly waving my arms to get his attention. I pointed at his feet and then mine.

He didn't comprehend my un-rehearsed signal and stood

like a ski-masked deer in the headlights, trying to understand what I meant.

I took off one of my sneakers and pointed to it—yet another unknown signal. I channeled my inner Speedy, the least-known and fastest dwarf, and ran. Richie sprinted behind me and tucked Sneezy safely away under a cloth tarp in the rafters of our garage.

All in all, our first night as juvenile cat burglars proved a success. We slipped into our twin beds with the rush of adrenaline still coursing through our veins.

In the room-lit glow of our nightlight, Richie reached down to the toes of his right foot and slid both hands up his ankle. He had just invented a new secret silent signal—*Next time, no stupid mistakes; black socks over white sneakers.*

Two weeks later, we spent the weekend at our family bungalow in Hampton Bays. My brother and I agreed that the Hamptons would be the ideal place to steal something—even though we had no idea what that something might be. (This is the key to understanding the vandal's mind. The only thing that matters is to get away with stealing something, anything. High-grade diamonds or oscillating lawn sprinklers—they're all the same to us.)

In late October, Hampton Bays was a sleepy ghost town. Vacationers had long since closed up their summer bungalows and migrated like the swallows of Capistrano back to Manhattan for the winter. Only a small population of local residents remained. They were on the same level of sophistication as Uncle Jed and Granny from the *Beverly Hillbillies* and were certainly no match for the city-smart burglar brothers Caragol. At least, that's what we told ourselves as a confidence builder.

After we arrived at the house on Friday night, my brother

and I watched *T.H.E. Cat* to pick up last-minute tips we might have missed in previous episodes.

We put on our ski masks, tucked an extra pair of black socks in our coat pockets, and said goodbye to our parents as we headed out the door for "a walk." I hugged Mom and Dad goodbye, not knowing if I would ever see them again. I imagined what life would be like in prison on the East River's Rikers Island and how much I would miss Mom's spaghetti and meatballs. One slip-up tonight and I'd be eating fried spam until my eventual execution on death row.

Richie and I wandered the dark, cottage-lined, salt air lanes of Hampton Bays, two aimless crooks in search of a caper. Neither of us had a crowbar or glass cutter or knew how to pick a lock, so we agreed that breaking into an unoccupied house was out of the question. Better to go with an *outdoor* burglary plan.

We thought of stealing lawn furniture but didn't know what we'd do with it since Hampton Bays was short on chaise-lounge fencing rings. Another option, garden tools, hardly seemed worth the risk. How embarrassing would it be to be arrested for first-degree trowel theft or grand rake larceny?

Just when Richie and I ran out of ideas, we arrived in front of the Tiana Bay Motel, listed in Fodor's as one of the world's great 1/32nd-of-One-Star resort destinations. The two-story blue cinderblock motel was closed for the winter and ripe for the picking. Other than one spotlight pointing at the motel sign at the entrance, the area was blacker than the socks covering our white sneakers.

"That's it," I whispered in my brother's ear. "The spotlights. We'll steal the spotlights and give 'em to the po-ah, ya know, the po-ah guys in my band." A noble cause indeed!

Spotlights weren't cheap. A decent set of color "spots," including back-ups, could easily wipe out six months of lawn-mowing money. But they were required gear for any teenage

'60s band that wanted to look like a real rock group instead of a bunch of acne-faced twerps playing under a basketball hoop in the school gymnasium. Big Brother and The Holding Company, Iron Butterfly, Hendrix—they all had light shows. The Tiana Bay Motel was our ticket to stardom, a virtual spotlight superstore with all the lights turned off.

The blue, red, yellow, and green spots were sound asleep after their summer of spraying splashes of color on walls, lawns, walkways, the swimming pool area, and the dock where cabin cruisers tied up for the night during peak season.

We went to work.

Richie silently crept up an outside staircase to the second-floor balcony, stepped onto the railing, and pulled himself up onto the flat tar-and-gravel roof. I assumed the position of lookout as my brother leaned over the rooftop on his belly, unscrewed bulbs, and stowed them inside a black pull-string laundry bag. If only our mother could have seen him. The bag, which she normally emptied of smelly shirts, socks, and Fruit of The Loom underwear, filled up fast with stolen goods.

In a matter of minutes, my feline frere bagged six spotlights. He waved me back up to the balcony and lowered the bag down to me from the roof. This was so easy. The booty bag could easily hold another dozen spots.

Emboldened by our rooftop operation, we ventured down the hill to the dock that stretched out into the bay. Mounted at the top of a 12-foot metal pole were three of the most beautiful spotlights I had ever seen—extra-large and sunflower yellow, the color of choice for repelling mosquitoes and disguising teenage rock band zits.

Once again, Richie did the hard work while I played the lookout. He shimmied up to the top of the pole and began to unscrew the first bulb—when we both saw it. Someone was coming our way, possibly a security guard, searching the grounds with a high-powered flashlight. The wide beam crisscrossed the lawn. He must have heard Richie walking on the roof.

Richie slid down the pole like a fireman rushing to a four-alarmer. We stood out in the open and would be seen in seconds.

He slipped under the dock with the booty bag.

I dove on the beach and tried to cover myself with a pile of seaweed. This was about as effective as hiding from a serial killer under a paper dinner napkin. The seaweed only concealed my legs. So I crawled turtle-style on all fours to a wooden rowboat lying upside down on the beach, lifted one side, and rolled under.

Through a small opening between the boat and the sand, I could see the flashlight beam scouring the beach. I heard heavy footsteps on the dock and pushed my face up to the opening under the boat to get a better look.

The tall stanger on the dock stood right above Richie. AND he held a GUN!

I couldn't risk sending Richie a secret hand signal, so I closed my eyes, concentrated, and used brain waves in a futile attempt to transmit a telepathic warning message: *Man holding gun. Do not move. Repeat. Do not move.*

Richie stood still in the waist-deep water. Man Holding Gun turned around and walked away. We waited until the coast was clear and darted home down the beach and through the woods.

Statistically speaking, we were two cats with seven spotlights and eight lives remaining.

You would think that Man Holding Gun scared us enough to end our criminal activities. It had the opposite effect. We believed we had experienced the worst-case scenario and passed the "Introduction to Burglary" test with flying colors. Spotlight schmotlight. We had bigger fish to steal.

Enter our "Tools and Tunes" shoplifting period.

While I've always been mechanically challenged, Richie had a gift for inventing, designing, and building things: motorbikes powered by rebuilt lawnmower engines, tree houses so elaborate they would have made Frank Lloyd Wright weep, three-foot-tall Estes model rockets fueled by cooking ingredients like baking soda, sugar, and horseradish.

One summer afternoon on our friend Robert's back porch, we leafed through *National Geographic Magazine* in search of pictures of topless tribeswomen. While flipping through the magazine, we found a feature article about the island of Tahiti. Within a few hours, Richie sketched a small ship that would sail us there. Fifteen years later, his ship appeared on the cover of *National Geographic*. I wondered how Jacques Cousteau had gotten hold of Richie's sketches and built The Calypso.

Richie was and is so visionary that I'm certain he could have built the first space shuttle in our basement workshop—if only he had the right tools.

To Richie, tools were far more than objects used to pound nails and saw wood. Tools were actualizers capable of making the pictures in his imagination become new working objects and mechanisms.

This single-minded passion drove Richie beyond random, senseless vandalism to the far more honorable pursuit of shoplifting tools used to help humankind, tools priced beyond his means but not beyond his magician-like hands and imagination.

He started small—a pocket-sized Allen Wrench set here, an all-in-one 17-tool Swiss army knife there. The old rusty pipe wrenches and splintered wooden claw hammers hanging above the basement workbench were gradually replaced by bright yellow-and-black Sears Craftsman contractor quality hammers, matching rubber-grip screwdriver shafts with interchangeable tool bits, and crescent wrenches of all sizes for turning everything from the tiny lug nuts on model racing car wheels to the water valve on a city fire hydrant.

I knew Richie had gone too far when he walked out of a Great Eastern Mills Department Store pushing a hand truck stacked with an industrial vice, gas-powered generator, and top-of-the-line table saw.

Meanwhile, I had developed a passion for music. I discovered the mind-expanding albums of Led Zeppelin, Steppenwolf, Jethro Tull, the Jimi Hendrix Experience, and Deep Purple while listening to the underground New York City rock station WOR in my bedroom on an iPhone-sized transistor radio.

Within a month of discovering my newfound love of all things rock, I traded my Stingray bicycle with a banana seat and high-rise handlebars for a cheap snare drum and cymbal. I cranked up the round volume dial on the side of my little radio and drummed along to "Light My Fire," "Smoke on The Water," and "Sunshine of Your Love."

I mowed lawns and pulled weeds all summer long to save enough money from my growing gardening business to buy a psychedelic iridescent drum set and a used Harman Kardon stereo system with a turntable.

When 8th grade started in September, I joined a band with three guitarists who, that summer, had mastered the seven chords necessary to play almost any hit song of the late 1960s.

I was on a life-altering music roll, and nothing could stop me except the money required to buy new albums and sheet music for the band.

In 1969, Richie's addiction to tools and my addiction to tunes collided during a shoplifting trip to Macy's.

Mrs. Hollingswood, friend Robert's mother, drove us to the Roosevelt Field Mall for an early evening shopping excursion.

While Mrs. H. and Robert headed to the Thom McAnn shoe store, Richie and I split off in the direction of Macy's.

We entered the store and went directly to the tool department, where Richie stuffed a plastic pack of iodized jigsaw blades down the back of his Lee dungarees. We rode the escalator up to the music department, where I pulled the sheet music for Black Sabbath's "Iron Man" off the rack and slipped it down the front of my white bell-bottom Levi's.

We rode back down the escalator and walked out of Macy's front door. Two huge hands gripped our shoulders from behind, and a deep, raspy, three-pack-a-day voice commanded in a heavy New York accent, "Come wit me, boys."

The burly undercover security guard caught us in the act. His neatly trimmed Joe Friday buzz cut and short-sleeved pale-blue dress shirt disguised his profession. He led us down to Macy's inner security sanctum, a small, dimly lit office in the basement furnished with a desk lamp and a cluttered desk piled high with stacks of folders containing reports on dozens of captured shoplifters.

Joe ordered us to sit in the two chairs in front of his desk and grilled us with questions. "First name? Middle initial? Last Name? Street address? City? Phone? Age? Criminal record? Next 'o kin?"

Joe leaned toward me after he filled out the "your life is over" forms and told me to stand up. He opened a desk drawer, pulled out an instant camera, and rolled down a shade on the office door marked with a seven-foot ruler. He told me to stand against the shade and face forward. Flash! He took my front mug shot, waited two minutes for the image to appear, and tacked it to a bulletin board displaying a gallery of shoplifter mug shots. He told me to turn left and posted my side profile on the board.

Richie's turn came next. Just before Joe pressed the camera button, Richie smiled in an ear-to-ear Cheshire Cat grin. Flash!

We were hosed. What was my brother thinking? Did he think the photos on the bulletin board looked way too serious and were in desperate need of comedic relief? Did he have it out for me and see this as the perfect time to take me down with him?

If Joe was upset, he didn't show it. He thumb-tacked both of my brother's white-bordered Polaroid photographs on the board next to mine. We were one sad and one ecstatic teenage shoplifter, side by side, among a photo exhibit of hardened adult criminals.

Joe ripped a photo of a young woman off the bulletin board. "Do ya see, huh?!! Do ya?" he shouted into our petrified faces with a gust of hot Chesterfield breath. "Yous are lucky my boss din't catch ya. He caught dis woman stealin' baby pajamas. She was nine munts pregnant when he sent huh to the slammuh."

I cried like a baby.

Richie promised we would never shoplift again.

Joe let us go.

Our brief life of crime was over. We had finally, mercifully, been demoted to T.H.E. Fraidy Cats.

16

NUCLEAR RATS ON PATROL

"Fluoridation is the most monstrously conceived
and dangerous communist plot we have ever had to face."
- General Jack D. Ripper, *Dr. Strangelove*

I n the early 1960s, the Rat Patrol of Long Island Boy Scout Troop #423 had a knot master, a cook, a medic, and nine goof-offs—including me—who were there mostly for the cool green khaki uniforms, parent-approved buck knives, and tent-farting contests. We followed the Scout motto, "Be Prepared." But nothing could have prepared my patrol for the elaborate Cuban Missile Crisis prank my brother and I concocted during a weekly Rat Patrol meeting in the basement of our house.

The Cold War was in full swing. We practiced "duck and cover" air raid drills under our desks at school. I don't know why this didn't put an end to nuclear weapon proliferation. We were told that ducking under a desk with our head between our knees would protect us from being blown up by a nuclear bomb. Didn't the Russians know that? I mean, what's the point of going to all the trouble and expense of dropping The Bomb when you can't even kill a sixth grader hiding under a flimsy school desk?

The ongoing threat of nuclear war with Russia put everyone on edge, including our guys in the Rat Patrol. We were constantly reminded by the media, military, parents, and teachers that Russia had missiles aimed at New York City. One touch of the red button and BOOM, it was all over.

Like the desert fighters in a popular TV show, *The Rat Patrol,* we fancied ourselves as a band of renegades. They were U.S. soldiers who fought Nazis in machine-gun jeeps in the sands of North Africa in WWII. We were U.S. Boy Scouts who fought boredom in the suburban sprawl of Long Island.

We took an oath to be helpful, trustworthy, clean, brave, loyal, and reverent in addition to six other socially redeeming principles—many in conflict with the ways of a teenage boy at the raging onslaught of puberty. Following all of the Boy Scout vows was certain to at least lead to being labeled a geek, and at most lead to having a seizure brought on by corking the natural boyhood impulse to be unhelpful, untrustworthy, unwashed, loyal only to a point, and as irreverent as a stand-up comic delivering the eulogy at a funeral.

More than a rite of passage, the Scouts presented an opportunity to play with matches, tie up your friends, pee in the woods, and buddy up under the stars in a tent full of boys engaged in the highly competitive sport of seeing who could expel the longest and loudest fart in the history of flatulence.

This popular Scout sport has yet to receive a merit badge, which is a shame since it requires tremendous skill, determination, and personal control.

Skinny Billy Grissom was our knot master. He knew how to tie a Double Half Hitch Yankee Slipknot under pressure in case we found ourselves hiking along a river during a sudden dam break and needed a quick rope bridge to cross over the oncoming wall of water.

Billy always came in first in the knot-tying race. Before the rest of us could lash up one shoelace bow, Billy could tie enough Sheepshanks to outfit a fleet of fishing schooners.

Jimmy Henry was the cook. Jimmy's unique cooking method involved defrosting frozen hot dogs over a bonfire slightly smaller than the one that burned Atlanta during Sherman's March to The Sea. During a winter camping trip to Bear Mountain in upstate New York, Jimmy's cook fire licked the limbs of a pine tree hanging 20 feet above the forest floor. As far as I know, our troop was the first in Scout history to extinguish a forest fire with snowballs.

Vito Forgioni received our unanimous vote for the medic. He came from a long line of Sicilians for whom the sight of blood was as common as a nice Chianti. He claimed that he "knew people" who could whack anybody who gave us problems. When Bobbie Kaminski sliced open his finger while whittling a stick with a Swiss Army knife, Vito calmly applied pressure to the wound with his kerchief while simultaneously shaking Bobbie's hand in a congratulatory gesture for taking it like a man.

The only procedure Vito refused to perform was mouth-to-mouth resuscitation. He made it clear that if any of us choked on a chicken bone, we were pretty much dead.

We met once a week during the school year to learn all the stuff a Scout needed to know, such as how to identify hundreds of birds, plants, and animals we would never encounter in the cement jungle of New York.

After several months of what became a drudgery of useless Scout activities, the time had come to liven things up.

The centerpiece of our basement was a 1940s mahogany radio cabinet the size of a top freezer. The console featured a big round backlit radio dial with AM frequency numbers, a turntable, a large cloth-covered speaker, and an amplifier filled with glass vacuum tubes.

Richie ran a hidden microphone cable from the back of the cabinet into an adjacent hollow bench that spanned the length of one wall, out the other side, behind the fake fireplace my mother purchased with Green Stamps, and under the door to the furnace room and workshop.

With a microphone in hand, my big brother could remotely broadcast an announcement through the radio cabinet from his secret workshop location, thus creating the illusion of a special emergency bulletin breaking into regular radio station programming.

Switching the dial on the stereo from "radio" to "turntable" in the middle of a radio program would cause the station to cut out and the microphone to cut in. A small window in the workshop afforded a full view of the finished part of the basement. This would allow Richie to see me at the exact moment I switched the dial so he could break into the radio music with a message from the Emergency Broadcasting System.

The fuse box, which controlled all the electricity in the house, was also in the workshop. This would provide the final hair-raising crescendo to our plot, loosely based on the "War of The Worlds" 1938 radio broadcast by Orson Wells that led thousands of listeners to believe that an alien attack on their homes was imminent.

On a Wednesday afternoon after school, all 12 members of The Rat Patrol assembled in my basement, dressed in uniform and ready to learn the next riveting page of knots in the Scout Handbook. I chose Wednesday afternoon for the meeting because that was when my mother always left the house on her weekly food-shopping trip to A&P. The only adult remaining in the house was our little old Norwegian housekeeper, Olga, who came to clean once a week and could barely speak a word of English.

The meeting began by reciting the Scout pledge. Jimmy The Cook then opened the traditional bag of Cheese Puffs, which would keep us nourished during the dull-as-dirt hour of knot tying. After everyone had taken a couple of hands full of the neon orange puffs, I placed the half-empty bag on top of the radio cabinet, turned it on, and tuned in to New York City's Top 40 station, WABC.

Vito The Medic, who was also the Patrol Leader, directed Billy "Knot Master" Grissom to demonstrate the correct procedure for tying an Overhand Cow Hitch.

We sat in a circle on the braided oval rug a few feet from the radio. Billy placed 12 ropes of equal length in the middle of the circle and explained that while the Cow Hitch was originally designed to tie a cow to a pole so it could graze freely, sailors later added the overhand knot at the loose end as a stopper that helped to secure a lanyard to a shroud.

He lost us at "stopper" but continued, expounding about the brilliance of the Overhand Cow Hitch as if it were on a par with such inventions as the light bulb and combustion engine. Billy was oblivious to the fact that none of us were, nor hoped to ever be, cattle ranchers or sailors. We just wanted to learn how to tie the goddamned knot so we could pass the merit badge test.

Vito came to the rescue. He threatened Billy with a Sicilian knee-capping if he didn't get on with the demonstration. Billy obliged.

A rush of excitement ran through me in anticipation of the hoax about to unfold. When everyone became fully engrossed in the technical loops of their Overhand Cow Hitches, I set the plan into action.

Stage 1: Moving unobtrusively out of the circle, I walked over to the stereo cabinet as WABC broadcasted the psychedelic song "My Green Tambourine."

Stage 2: I grabbed the Cheese Puffs off the top of the cabinet as a diversionary tactic and simultaneously flipped the amplifier knob from "radio" to "turntable." The music cut out, followed by several seconds of silence. Vito yelled, "Hey, what the fuck happened to the music?" I answered, "Beats me. It just stopped."

Stage 3: A voice erupted from the radio cabinet.

"THIS IS AN IMPORTANT MESSAGE FROM THE EMERGENCY BROADCASTING SYSTEM. THIS IS NOT A TEST. I REPEAT. THIS IS NOT A TEST.

Scouts turned and leaned toward the radio.

"THE PENTAGON HAS JUST ANNOUNCED THAT RUSSIA AND CHINA HAVE LAUNCHED NUCLEAR MISSILES TARGETED AT THE NEW YORK METROPOLITAN AREA.

Scouts looked toward each other, confused. Vito The Medic cursed in disbelief, "Russia AND China? Fuckin' 'eh! How is that fuckin' possible? Fuck!!"

"THE MISSILES WERE LAUNCHED FROM A JOINT RUSSIAN AND CHINESE BASE ON THE ISLAND OF CUBA AT 4:00 PM, EASTERN STANDARD TIME.

The clock on the wall read 4:10. The basement exploded in Boy Scout bedlam.

"ALL RESIDENTS IN THE NEW YORK, NEW JERSEY, CONNECTICUT, AND PENNSYLVANIA AREA ARE ADVISED TO GO TO THE NEAREST AIR RAID SHELTER OR INTO YOUR BASEMENT IMMEDIATELY.

Jimmy barfed up his Cheese Puffs.

"THE ESTIMATED TIME OF IMPACT IS..."

Stage 4: In the workshop, Richie furiously unscrewed fuses. The radio cut out. The basement plunged into darkness. The Rat Patrol unraveled. Some screamed. One guy slid under the coffee table. Another rocked back and forth on the rug, whimpering, "No, no, no, no." Vito The Medic yelled, "Duck and cover! Fuckin' duck!"

The commotion alarmed Olga, who was upstairs vacuuming when the power in the house cut out. I looked up and
saw her shadow standing on the landing at the top of the basement stairs, shaking her fists and shouting, "Hurddie gurdy ber
der vimentin farvold gurdy hurddie!!!" I didn't understand
Norwegian. I assumed she meant, "Holy crap! What's happen-
ing?" Her vacuum had stopped working, and she was alone in a
house full of screaming Boy Scouts. The practical joke had
gone too far. It was too practical, too believable, and no longer a
joke.

I stumbled in the dark, tripping over Scouts huddled in
fetal positions on the floor, and finally crawled on all fours
toward the workshop to call off the joke.

Meanwhile, Richie feverishly screwed and unscrewed the
fuse that controlled the electricity in the basement—even
though we never discussed flickering lights in Stage 4. The
lights flashed on and off, adding yet another layer of terror to
the end-of-the-world scenario.

Now crying out in sheer terror, The Rat Patrol presumed
that the nuclear storm had wreaked havoc upon the New York
electrical grid. Any second, we all would all be toasted into
human X-rays.

I reached the workshop door on my hands and knees,
turned the handle, and pushed. Inside, Richie appeared and
disappeared as the lights flashed on and off. He stood at the
fuse box, completely absorbed in the act of playing with electricity.

In the flickering light, he resembled a teenage Dr. Frankenstein conducting a freakish experiment during a lightning
storm. I yelled at the top of my lungs, "Richie! Stop! They-ah
goin' crazy!"

When Richie finally heard me and set the fuses back to
their fully locked positions, I was so distressed that I kept

screaming when the lights stayed on, "Stop! Stop! They think it's real! We went too fah! Stop!"

The eyes of 11 Scouts bored down on me. They heard every word I screamed to my brother. I had divulged our secret prank to a basement of stunned Tenderfeet, haphazardly strewn across the floor, armed with buck knives and enough Overhand Cow Hitch rope to hang my brother and me.

Vito yelled, "Get the fucker!"

Richie slammed and locked the workshop door. Eleven enraged Boy Scouts charged in a unified frontal attack. I was being crushed under a 1,500-lb. pile of green khaki.

"Hurdee gurdy tooksa bjorndig spaten plotzon!" Olga screamed as she pulled one Rat after another off the pile.

I rolled over on my back and saw her waving her arms and dispersing the mob with a barrage of threats in Norwegian that only she understood. Nevertheless, it had the effect of diffusing all the tension in the room, which quickly erupted into uncontrollable laughter when Olga marched back up the basement stairs shouting, "Golgle chpeck hoozle droodooble maplazoo." Which I later discovered meant, "Wait until your mother gets home."

Rats.

17

THE OBLIVIOUS BUSBOY
CHRONICLES

"I was so naïve as a kid I used to
sneak behind the barn and do nothing."
- Johnny Carson

"I SWAY-AH I DIN'T DO IT! I DIN'T PUT THE COCKROACH IN THE SHRIMP COCKTAIL! I JUST SERVED IT TO THE LADY AND THEN SHE SCREAMED! YOU SHOULDA SEEN IT! THE COCKROACH CRAWLED OUT FROM UNDER THE COCKTAIL SAUCE! I DON'T KNOW HOW IT GOT IN THEY-AH! HONEST!"

Loretta, the brassy head waitress, didn't believe a word I said. A dead-ringer for the evil sister of Ichabod Crane, she had caught dozens of busboys making mischief over the years. She passed my guilty verdict without a second thought. I would either be fired or forced to serve 90 days of busboy probation under her scrutinizing eyes.

Loretta slowly slipped the rhinestone eyeglasses off her long, pointy nose. Her icy glare petrified me. Her poofy beehive hairdo tilted forward as she leaned in to drive home her point. "This better not happen again. Get to work, Shrimp Boat."

Ugh, work. If that's what people did to earn money until the day they ended up in a nursing home, I would rather have tried my hand as a petty thief.

As ill fate would have it, Loretta didn't fire me. I worked as a busboy that whole summer at the Hampton Bays Diner. The silver whale-of-a-restaurant on Eastern Long Island was a popular gathering place for locals as well as celebrities like Marilyn Monroe and Paul Newman.

This is where I first became the test dummy for other people's practical jokes. Picking on the naive and scatterbrained new kid didn't require a doctorate in Advanced Trickery. Even an intellectually deficient nincompoop could have done it. Case in point—Johnny Signano—a fellow busboy who set me up in the *Cockroach-in-the-Shrimp-Cocktail* incident. Johnny resembled a young John Belushi who would have fit in perfectly with the troublemakers in *Animal House*.

After Loretta Queen-of-the-Wait-Staff bawled me out, Johnny laughed his face off. He pretended to wipe down a table that was already set for the next dinner guests, a dead giveaway that he was the shrimp cocktail saboteur.

I decided not to rat him out. I had to work with this jokester and didn't want to throw napalm on the fire. If Johnny had marked me as a snitch, he would have probably upped his game. A sink full of 300-degree cooking oil when it's my turn to wash dishes? Locking me in the walk-in freezer until my fingers and toes froze blue and snapped off? Substituting Gravy Train for beef stew when I took my meal break in the kitchen?

As Michael Corleone said in *The Godfather*, "Keep your friends close and your enemies closer." I befriended Johnny Signano. We became summer buddies. Johnny took me under his wing. He taught me how to orchestrate simple yet diabolical pranks on obnoxious patrons.

Busboys and waitresses were on high alert every night between 9:30 and midnight, the dreaded period known as "Bar

Break." Packs of loaded college students poured into the diner to get some food in their bellies and sober up after consuming massive quantities of Rheingold beer and Jim Beam shots at the local bars.

One night, a group of six over-served college guys stumbled through the door singing "The Chapel of Love." The hostess led them to a booth in the back room. They proceeded to challenge each other to a catsup bottle chugging contest. They whistled cat calls at waitresses. They burped the alphabet in unison, possibly imagining themselves performing on stage for an equally drunk audience of belching concertgoers.

Johnny winked at me. I was ready to watch the master at work. Whatever Johnny had up his sleeve was going to be good.

He filled six water glasses. Rather than carry them to the table on a tray, he plunged his fingers into the glasses and squeezed them together, three in each hand, resembling two water-glass chandeliers hanging from his fingertips.

Johnny plunked the glasses on the table and performed his coup de gras. He wiped his nose with his hands, slipped his fingers back into the glasses, and slid them across the table like hockey pucks across an ice rink. The glasses landed perfectly in front of all six drunks. That shut them up. Johnny bowed, turned, and walked away. Nearby tables applauded and cheered.

The meal didn't sober up those college kids. Johnny did.

That summer, Johnny built a go-cart, affectionately called "The Death Trap." His design featured an iron frame of long green garden stakes bolted together, a 1963 Ford Falcon steering wheel from a wrecking yard, a Briggs and Stratton 12 horsepower engine, a driver seat duct-taped together with torn lawn chair cushions, and a razor-sharp exhaust pipe.

The go-cart gave us weeks of boyhood thrills. Johnny, Richie, and I took turns racing up and down the sandy street in front of the Signano's bungalow on the bay.

Jump-starting the engine required a seamless sequence of actions by the driver. At the end of about our 20th race day, I assumed the starting position, standing beside the cart. I pushed it while running, pressed the starter button on the engine, and hopped in behind the wheel. It went like clockwork. I raced down the street, jumped the dune, completed a figure eight on the rocky beach below, and sped back like a wannabe Mario Andretti.

The Hampton 500 ended in a dash to the finish line, a bright yellow boat line stretched across the street between two mailbox posts. I beat the record of three minutes and sixteen seconds, jumped out of the go-cart, and raised my arms in a V-for-victory pose.

Unfortunately, my leg went down in defeat.

Johnny was the first to see it. The sharp exhaust pipe sliced open my right calf like a pork loin when I ran to jump-start the engine. It cut through the muscle over and over with each leg lunge. Richie looked at the gaping wedge of exposed calf muscle and decided what we should do. "That doesn't look good. Let's ride home. Mom'll know what to do."

On the five-mile bike ride home, I convinced Richie not to mention the wound. I'd heard about stitches and wanted to avoid the pain. My powers of persuasion dissolved after I limped into the house. Mom asked, "Philip, why are yah limpin'?" Richie answered, "He sliced his leg open! It looks really bad! He probably needs stitches!"

She drove us straight to the hospital in South Hampton. Twenty-three stitches later, the emergency room released me. I was good to go. But under Mom's orders, "go" no longer included the "go" in go-cart.

Other than my cousin Willie and Rita Moreno in *West Side Story*, I'd never met Puerto Ricans in my youth. The movie starred a bunch of white guys who were anything but Puerto Rican. Actors with names like George Chakiris (Greek), Robert Thompson (British), and Larry Roquemore (French) played the "Sharks" gang. They were about as Puerto Rican as Mister Rogers.

My perception of the people of Puerto Rico changed in the summer of 1968. The kitchen at the diner might as well have been dubbed *Pico Puerto Rico*. About a dozen amigos made the kitchen hum. They were sous chefs, fry cooks, salad makers, potato mashers, dishwashers, and trash haulers. They worked hard. And festively.

These guys didn't just *move* around the kitchen. They *danced*, sometimes in a swaying conga line from the cooler to the griddle. The lively beats of Salsa, Bomba, and Merengue filled the kitchen and helped the crew to keep the meals coming.

On more than one occasion, I joined *mi amigos* jam sessions out on the loading dock. They didn't own instruments except for a beat-up acoustic guitar they rescued from the garbage dump. So, they improvised.

The brass section blew kazoos. Conga players drummed on cardboard produce cartons with big wooden spoons. Scratching a fork across the surface of a cheese grater made the perfect *güira*, adding percussive Latin flair.

But the most coveted instrument, by far, was the horn in the diner's old rusty garbage truck. They took turns behind the wheel. One song per man gave each player the chance to beep-beep-beep their own signature truck horn solo. The music and energy exploded on that loading dock. Until then, I had no idea that adults could be so much fun.

Thanks to our island *amigos*, the diner turned out to be more of a cultural awakening than a job. Chico taught me my first Spanish phrases, all curse words and filthy insults involving someone's sister or mother. Fernando, who spoke conversational English, counseled me in matters not yet understood by a 15-year-old boy-man—girls, bullies, moderation, money, and homespun acne treatments from the Caribbean.

Fernando was a superb mentor. He spoke his mind, directly connected to his mouth with no filter in between.

One day, I asked my mother if she would pick up me, my brother, and Fernando at the diner. He missed the ocean and didn't own a car to drive to the ocean beach. She felt compassion for him and agreed to take us to a relaxing afternoon on the sugar sands of the Hamptons.

Fernando sat in the front passenger seat. On the drive there, he turned to my mother and fired off a string of questions.

"How much you pay for car?"

"Womans ok to drive in Amereeca, *si*?"

"You like me teach you how to cook *Mofongo*?"

For a second, I thought Fernando let slip one of Chico's filthy phrases directed at my mother. Then it occurred to me that Mom didn't speak Spanish, so she wouldn't have been insulted anyway.

Ever polite, she answered his questions with grace, even though driving a stranger with her boys in the car fell way outside her comfort zone. She chuckled and smiled as Fernando turned on the charm and slowly put her at ease. That said, his next question catapulted our mother out of her comfort zone.

"*Senorita* Caragol, eef a man break into you house, ees ok to shoot him, *si*?"

I thought, *Holy Mofongo mom's not going to like that question.*

Mi madre gripped the steering wheel. Her soft green eyes hardened with the alertness of someone about to be murdered, or more specifically, someone who had just picked up an apparent serial killer from the tropical island of Puerto Rico.

My brother saved the day. Richie leaned over the front seat and whispered into Fernando's ear. "You're scaring her. No more questions about shooting people."

Fernando nodded, signaling that he had received the message. "*Senorita* Caragol, I never own a gun. But eef I did, I would use to protect you and your familia. You are, how you say, nice womans. You *una buena* driver, too."

Mom's shoulders relaxed. We dodged a Puerto Rican bullet. My mother listened attentively from the driver's seat as Fernando recited the recipe for *Mofongo*. As far as I could tell, the ingredients didn't include any distasteful words about my sister or *Mom-fongo*.

***

Waitresses at the diner were mostly high school and college girls looking for a summer job near the beach. The Carey sisters were among them. Rita, 19, and Erin, 16, were townies who grew up in Hampton Bays. Both redheads had a wicked sense of humor. The Carey sisters were a force to be reckoned with, and I reckoned that my first summer romance with Erin would be a dream come true.

Sure, she was older. She could have her pick of guys who were more mature and better looking. But I was a naïve teenage busboy. The world was my oyster. Or so I thought until the night the Carey sisters picked me for their oyster and pried me open at a beach house party.

A group of waitresses rented an old, run-down six-bedroom house perched on a bluff overlooking Peconic Bay. They hosted a summer bash for the diner's staff. To my astonishment, Mom allowed my brother and me to go. I'd never been to an unsupervised party with college kids and had no idea what to expect.

Rita and Erin gave us a lift to the party directly after work on a humid August night. Rita drove her cherry-red Ford Fairlane convertible like a maniac. She rode the backroads so we could weave back and forth across the double yellow lines without cops around. When the band The Strawberry Alarm Clock played on the radio, she cranked up their hit song "Incense and Peppermints" to a volume level known in the future as *Spinal Tap II*.

The Carey sisters swayed left and right with the swerving motion of the convertible. From our vantage point in the back seat, they looked not unlike two Irish Setters out for an evening drive, the ruffs of their flowing red hair streaming backward in the salt air.

When we arrived at the party, the sunset cast an eerie orange glow on the decrepit house, the spitting image of *The Addams Family* mansion. Blaring music, bluish clouds of cigarette smoke, and the sounds of commotion poured out of the windows. Richie and I were about to enter a foreign world where beers were found, and inhibitions lost.

A crushed can of Schlitz beer sailed past our heads as we stepped through the doorway and crossed the threshold into mayhem. Couples danced wildly, bathed in the surreal indigo glow of colored bulbs in the floor lamps. They contorted their bodies in positions never intended for the *Homo erectus* frame. *Human Slinkies* came to mind, a gyrating mass of swirling hips and flailing arms contorted at odd angles.

Rita and Erin led us to the kitchen. Illuminated with another lighting color, I assumed it to be "the green room," an accurate description of how the kitchen crowd might feel the next morning. Two college girls stood on chairs; one held a bottle of scotch, the other a bottle of soda. A limbo line slinked between them as the girls poured scotch and sodas into the open mouths of the bent-backward dancers.

The Carey sisters reached into the refrigerator and offered

us cans of Schlitz. Richie and I didn't want to appear like the unsophisticated teenagers we were, so we peeled off the red pop tops and took a long swig. The suds erupted in my mouth. Foam oozed from the corners of my mouth like a rabid cocker spaniel. Not a good impression for a summer romance with Erin. I thought, *I'm Mofongoed.*

The first beer of my life tasted absolutely foul. My brain and mouth suffered a major disconnect. I expected beer to taste sweet and bubbly, sort of like a Canada Dry ginger ale. Yech! Why would anyone drink something that tasted like an effervescent form of stale bread?

About four gulps in, I began to understand the allure of ale.

Beer was no ordinary beverage. I rose to a heightened sense of awareness. Not just awareness of Erin and Rita, but I felt connected to everyone and everything—the music, the foul odor of hops, sweat, and cigarette smoke.

I one-beer-believed that everything I'd done and the scatterbrained challenges I'd faced up until then had prepared me for this aha moment. I had crossed the Grand Canyon between boyhood and manhood. The universe had designated that very night as my official adulthood coming-out party.

Erin ushered me into the living room. The dance party had escalated. I left my adolescent cocoon and emerged as a social butterfly. I, too, morphed into a Human Slinky with dance moves that might have easily been mistaken for a grand mal seizure.

Erin and I sprang from the floor to the couch to the coffee table as if we re-enacted the mating ritual of cheetahs. It became clear to me that we had fallen in love at some undefinable split-second leap between the coffee table and the walnut GE TV console.

Rita interrupted what could have been the best summer romance since *Splendor in the Grass*. She shouted something to Erin. I couldn't hear her over the stereo system blasting

"Gimme Gimme Some Lovin'.". The next thing I knew, the Carey sisters led me upstairs. I went along for the ride, presumably safer than our drive in Rita's Fairlane.

The Carey sisters creaked open a battered, paint-chipped door at the top of the stairs. Rita closed and locked the door behind us. The three of us were in a large bedroom bathed in yet another lighting color. According to my recent experiences in the green and blue rooms, I assumed that Rita, Erin, and I were together, alone, in the red room.

The euphoria brought on by the beer began to fade. I was trapped in the red-light district of the *Addams Family* mansion, sweating teen boy bullets. Why did the Carey sisters bring me to a bedroom? What did they expect from me? I had no experience in intimate relations with one person, no less two, not to mention TWO SISTERS.

Rita slinked toward me. "Phil, we've been keeping an eye on you."

Erin joined in. "Phil, we think you're dreamy."

"We want to get to know you better," Rita whispered in my ear.

"MUCH better," Erin exhaled, so close that the warmth of her breath danced across my lips.

Rita unbuttoned my sauce-stained busboy shirt. Erin rubbed her palms across my chest. My heart pounded. A kiss was one thing. That's all I hoped for: the dawn of a summer romance with Erin. But this was too much. The red-haired sisters pushed me over the cliff of adolescent insecurity.

I panicked, darted out of the room, and scrambled down the stairs, skipping steps. I searched the house and finally found Richie outside, swaying on the back porch swing with Marla, a wholesome University of Connecticut sophomore that my brother had a crush on ever since he first laid eyes on her at the diner. They were both introverts and snuck outside to get away from the crowd.

"Richie! Richie! Ya won't believe what just happened to me. We hafta leave!"

"Leave?" Richie replied in a love-struck voice. "I'm not ready to go yet. And besides, we don't have a ride home until Rita's ready to split."

When Richie finished making his point, Fernando miraculously appeared out of the shadows. "*Hola mi amigos*. I borrowed *un coche*. Eet is called a Plee-mouth Furious. Would you like ride *a su casa*?"

I pulled Richie aside and told him what had happened in the red-light room with the Carey sisters. My big brother reluctantly acquiesced. He gave Marla a goodnight butterfly kiss on the cheek.

We slid onto the front bench seat of Fernando's borrowed car and headed home. I hung my head out of the window and gazed up at the Little Dipper. I re-played scenes in my head from the night that changed my life.

I came close to crossing a double yellow line with the Carey sisters. Or were they just messing with me? I decided to stick with the double yellow line theory, at least for the moment, with the cool wind blowing through my hair like a happy puppy who had almost performed *Mofongo*.

———

The summer season at the diner ended with an unexpected and humiliating learning curve during the annual tradition known to some (except me) as "D-Day." No one took the minute or so it might have cost them to fill me in about "Diner Day," nor my debut in its starring role.

D-Day arrived on the Sunday before Labor Day, the last day before we ran out of summertime. By Labor Day Monday, our carefree vacation lives would be put on hold until next year. Vacationers would pack their behemoth car trunks, start their sad engines, and drive home droopy-faced in bumper-to-bumper traffic back to Nassau, Queens, or Manhattan and ordinary life.

On D-Day 1968, the breakfast shift was as slow as molasses. A few early-bird locals ordered the usual crab omelet or the classic eggs and bacon with hashbrowns, toast, and a bowl of the freshest peaches money could buy from a Number 10 tin can.

By sunset, a line stretched out the front door into the packed parking lot. The diner was the last stop before the on-ramp of the dreaded highway back to reality. The meal gave vacation evacuees a final break before serving months caged inside the four walls of their offices or classrooms.

The chatter of the dinner crowd faded when a song, unlike any we'd heard, played over the speaker system. It was a New York radio broadcast of the U.S. release of "Hey Jude." Diners lowered their forks and listened. Waitresses paused in the middle of scribbling orders. I quietly lowered a stack of dirty plates into a dish tub and stared up at the speaker in the ceiling.

The Beatles "Hey Jude" gave us the words we needed to describe how we felt about each other and the end of our time together that summer—*don't make it bad, take a sad song and make it better, better, better, better, OH!*

When "Hey Jude" reached its climax, a conga line of kitchen *amigos* burst through the double doors behind the counter. I hopped on the back of the line and grabbed hold of Fernando's waist. I loosely translated his ecstatic expression as some version of "*Viva Amereeca, Señor Jude!*"

Tables of college kids, families, and couples stood up and joined the conga line, followed by busboys, waitresses, and even stodgy old Loretta. We snaked through the restaurant like a diner choir, dancing and singing *Na, na, na, nananana, nananana, Hey Jude!*

It was a glorious finale to our summer vacation. Except for one small *Mofongo*.

When "Hey Jude" ended, the whole diner cheered and then went back to business as usual. "Usual," except for my D-Day debut as the diner's oblivious village idiot.

The Carey sisters cornered me in the men's room. With my back against the stall, I started to fret. *What if they lock the door and have their way with me? What if we get caught and my parents find out? I'll be grounded for a month, or worse yet, ordered to apologize to the Carey sisters' parents.*

My worries evaporated when Rita and Erin told me their intentions. Of all the people they could have chosen, they picked me to be the year's official D-Day busboy.

Rita blurted out the news. "Phil. We all voted, and you're the one everybody wants to throw the chocolate cream pie this year!" Erin backed her up. "What an honor, Phil! Isn't that exciting? You must be super proud!"

Actually, I was super confused and asked, "Throw the pie?" "Oh, you don't know?" said Rita.

"You're kidding, right? It's the best diner tradition ever!" declared Erin. "Every year, we pick a new busboy to throw a chocolate cream pie in Loretta's face. Just wait until she comes into the front room, and wham! Everybody will be watching. It's gonna be a blast. And you'll be our D-Day hero!"

"Wait", I said. "Do ya mean to tell me Loretta doesn't mind? She gets hit in the face with a pie every year, and she's OK with dat?"

"OK?" they chirped in unison. "She loves it!"

We snuck out of the men's room and returned to the front room. Guests occupied every booth and counter stool. Rita slipped behind the counter and handed me a cream pie from the glass dessert case. She whispered instructions. "Stay right here and look busy. Loretta's in the kitchen. When she comes out, let her have it. We'll all be waiting. You're gonna love this, and so will she. You're on."

I had a bad feeling, kind of like being blindfolded in front of a waitress firing squad. My knees weakened. I palmed the pie in my throwing hand and wiped down the counter with my other hand, trying to look busy. I waited for Loretta to appear through the swinging kitchen doors and noticed all of the waitresses hovering for a front-row view of the pie toss. They also tried to look busy. Just another normal shift at the diner. Nothing to see here.

Loretta didn't come through the kitchen doors. She entered through the far dining room and caught me by surprise. My D-Day moment had arrived. It was now or never.

When Loretta reached the counter, I addressed her with the cheerful greeting, "Hi Loretta! Happy D-Day!" She cocked her head as if to say, *Happy what?* But it was too late. The cream pie had already left my hand and flew through the air between us in what appeared to be a slow-motion horror scene. The pie hit Loretta square in the face with her mouth open.

The pie pan slid down her face and bounced on the floor. Her white waitress blouse and skirt were splattered with globs of gooey chocolate. Loretta couldn't speak. Or see. A thick mask of whipped cream covered her face, her swoopy rhinestone glasses, and the front slope of her bouffant hairdo.

The entire restaurant gasped as Loretta removed her glasses, unmasking the only part of her face not covered in whipped cream. A sculptor could not have carved such a perfect recessed mold of her wing-tipped glasses, surrounded by a field of creamy white.

Startled, stupefied, and seething, Loretta stormed past me. All eyes followed her as she shoved open the kitchen batwing doors, and they swung behind her. Then all eyes turned on me, the despicable busboy. I froze, acutely aware that I had just become the bad lead actor in a D-Day assault with a creamy weapon.

Waitresses scattered. Rita and Erin sheepishly approached me, cleaned up the mess on the floor, and walked away.

The only one who hung in there with me was friend and prank instructor Johnny Signano.

He stood by the front doors and quietly clapped his hands as if to say, *You have learned well, Mofongo.*

✣ 18 ✣
EYE KISS YOU

"Kissing can be a lot like songwriting—sometimes it's spontaneous
and magical, other times, you're left wondering
what you were thinking."
- John Lennon

P uberty ruins childhood. Once teenage hormones kick
in, there's no turning back. Out of nowhere, I started
having "thoughts" about girls. I anxiously wondered,
What if I try to kiss her and she laughs? What if I lose my nerve?
What if I forget to close my eyes and look like I'm in a state of shock?
My questions were soon answered in the most awkward way.

Life was innocent and so much simpler before I reached
adolescence and transformed into hormones in sneakers.
Starting at age 13, I wasn't afraid of many things. Kissing a girl
for the first time pretty much topped the list.

That first kiss meant way more than pressing my lips
against hers. The first kiss was a slippery slope, a love bridge to
the future. One kiss might lead to another with the same girl,
another junior high romance, or my future wife.

Guy friends were no help. My macho Long Island buddies

told me, "Don't think about it. Just kiss her!" Easy for them to say. I had so many questions but was too embarrassed to ask. My naïve questions could have been seen as a sign that I was an immature rookie with zero experience. Which was true.

Research helped. I watched old black-and-white romance movies. Cary Grant kissed Audrey Hepburn in *Charades,* and she went all googly-eyed. Kissing looked to be the number one thing couples did when they fell in love.

To my frustration, film censors back then limited the on-screen kiss to a few seconds—not nearly enough time to memorize winning kissing techniques. If only we had streaming TV channels in 1966. I would have been able to pause > rewind > play > fast forward > pause> play the perfect kiss and had enough time left over to draw detailed anatomical sketches.

I ramped up my research over the summer. At the ocean beach, approximately every fourth blanket was a horizontal kissing booth. High school and college couples in swimsuits lying side by side, made out with wild abandon and dripped with beads of sweat or salt water. It was hard to tell the difference from a distance.

I strolled down the beach, waves crashing, and spied a couple I dubbed Frankie and Annette lip-locked under a rainbow beach umbrella. Frankie's back blocked my view of the long, slow kiss he planted on Annette. I needed a closer look, but I couldn't exactly walk over, sit on their blanket, and announce, "Hi, I'm just doin' some research. Ignaw me and enjoy yaw heavy-breathin'."

I had to observe them without being obvious and saw that the best viewing spot was atop the dunes behind them. I snuck around Frankie and Annette, climbed the dunes, and hid in the high beach grass to conduct my research. The birds-eye view paid off as I watched the two lovers engrossed in what I assumed to be a case study in best-practice kissing.

Unfortunately, my hiding spot turned out to be not so hidden. Muscular Frankie caught me watching. I was a doomed Peeping Phil. He sprang off the blanket and chased me over the dunes, through the parking lot, and around the beach chalet housing a snack bar, bathrooms, showers, changing rooms, and a surfboard rental shop. I hid behind a wall of upright surfboards until Frankie gave up and ran back to Annette.

As luck would have it, the blonde-haired surf shop guy and his girlfriend were making out behind the counter. I had finally witnessed the perfect kiss close up in Sam Peckinpah slow motion. Gentle lips upon lips. Small caresses. Arms wrapped around each other in a sweet embrace. That was a kiss. That was love. That was the research finding that had eluded me.

From that point forward, the only thing holding me back was the perfect moment with the perfect girl. Her name was Theresa Tutunic.

I met Theresa in my freshman year of high school. Although her last name sounded like the luxury cruise ship that sank to the bottom of the North Atlantic, we enjoyed each other's company.

Theresa's golden shoulder-length hair, dimpled cheeks, and glowing smile made me stupidly happy. She laughed at my idiotic jokes. I applauded her quick wit and clever comebacks. We held hands walking around the block but still hadn't taken the first step to lip-to-lip euphoria.

It took meticulous planning to orchestrate my first kiss with Theresa. My current and future love life depended on it.

Enter The Squires Friday night dance. I joined The Squires with about a dozen other buddies in junior high. We were the adolescent version of the adult men's Knights of Columbus. It's one of the world's largest fraternal service organizations named in honor of Christopher Columbus, who unknowingly passed the plague on to first-nation Americans and kissed their asses goodbye.

The Knights performed good works for millions of people in need. And you couldn't beat their ceremonial outfit—navy blue tuxedo; red, white, and blue silk sash; sweeping red cape; sparkling sword hung at the waist; and a black double-billed military hat topped with a fluffy plume of white feathers.

The Knights owned a two-story brick building with a full bar, billiards room, and dance hall. We Squires held some of the best school dances in town with local bands that played Top-40 songs from bands of the '60s—Herman's Hermits, The Beach Boys, The Righteous Brothers, The Rascals, The Four Seasons, The Turtles, Paul Revere and The Raiders, The Beatles, The Stones, Steppenwolf.

I invited Theresa to the dance. The hall was packed. Boys and girls gyrated to "Born to Be Wild," then swayed in a full-body-hug slow dance to "Cherish." It was during "Cherish" that I came close to making out with Theresa. She nuzzled her face into the crook of my neck. Her curls, the color of wheat, cascaded down my shoulder. She wrapped her arms around me. I reciprocated. We pressed our bodies together in a heart-throbbing embrace.

I had conducted extensive research for this moment. I was ready. The music swept us into a tingling cloud of boy-girl bliss. She lifted her head from my shoulder. Our eyes met. Our souls connected. She exhaled a deep breath and puckered her lips in anticipation of a passionate kiss.

I almost gagged. Theresa Tutunic's foul breath ruined any chance that our lips would touch that night.

As charming and beautiful as she was, genetics cursed her with a horrible case of halitosis. Her breath was bad enough to awaken the nasal senses of men deprived of olfactory perception from birth. The invisible gust of poison air billowing from her lips could have stopped a charging rhino.

I excused myself and stepped outside for a breath of fresh air. I yearned to kiss Theresa with every fiber of my being, but it would have to wait. Offering her breath mints would be rude and also kill the mood.

Next time, I would simply steal a kiss as quickly as possible while holding my breath like a free diver in the nauseating aroma of a low-tide lagoon.

The moment had finally arrived to kiss Theresa. We Squires locked in the plan for our date-night make-out party in our clubhouse below the Knights of Columbus hall. The basement space featured a shuffleboard table, jukebox, floor lamps, cushy chairs, couches, and cement walls decorated with posters of Christopher Columbus, Three Dog Night, and NY Jets star quarterback Joe Namath.

My dad drove me to Theresa's house on the east side of town. Her mother greeted me at the door with specific instructions to bring her only daughter home no later than 10 o'clock. That gave me three hours to work up the nerve to kiss her while holding my breath.

Dad dropped us off at the hall. We walked down the back stairs into The Squire's den. It was only 7:00 and the make-out party was already in full swing.

The jukebox played steamy songs by the Classics IV. "Stormy," "Spooky," and "Traces" set the mood for major necking. Boys and girls embraced on the green shag carpet, plush plaid sofas, and loveseats. Blue spotlights reflected off the low ceiling cast the basement in a smoldering junior-high sex vibe.

The love den was so crowded that only one empty place remained for Theresa and me to hopefully make out—the shuffleboard table, covered in sawdust. It was a long, narrow game table on which two players slid metal pucks to score points, or, in our case, where two teenagers slid together to score a kiss.

I lifted Theresa onto the table, her legs dangling above the floor. I climbed up next to her, my legs and confidence dangling precipitously in expectation of my first failed or successful kiss.

We exchanged nervous small talk.

"Great music, Phil!"

"Have ya evva played shuffleboard?"

"Gee, it's so dark in here."

"Do ya think the Jets'll beat the Steeluhs on Sunday?"

"Geeze, how'll I get all this sawdust off my skirt?"

Enough was enough. It was now or never. I inhaled, held my breath, and turned as fast as I could to kiss Theresa and get it over with before I lost my nerve.

I miscalculated and kissed her in the eye.

She couldn't compose herself. In the silent airspace between the songs "All My Lovin'" and "Sealed with A Kiss," Theresa covered her right eye with her palm and yelled, "My eye! I can't believe you kissed me in my eye!"

The basement erupted in howling laughter. My first attempted kiss with the Tutunic went down like a shipwreck.

For a self-esteem booster, I told myself that I *did* successfully manage to avoid inhaling Theresa's funky breath, and a better kiss awaited me somewhere, sometime with someone on the distant hormone horizon.

❧ 19 ❧
DON'T FORCE ZA MOLTS!

"I'm sorry there is no ice cream, Herr General.
We had pistachio, but one of the guards shot it with a machine
gun."
- Colonel Klink, *Hogan's Heroes*

I worked at Beier's German Restaurant and Ice Cream Parlor in my junior and senior years of high school. It seemed like a good place to make enough money to cover my increasing teenage expenses—until the day I was forced to work under the iron fist of Henry, whom I still suspect was the go-to chocolatier of Hitler and the Nazi party.

You might call Beier's one of the early destination restaurants. The owner, 62-year-old Mr. Moppel, enlisted the help of Henry, an old, crotchety confectioner with beady eyes and a guttural German accent. He made the most buttery-delicious chocolate Easter bunnies in the five-borough NYC area. Jesus, they were good. Even Jewish neighbors came in to buy them during Passover.

Beier's ice cream was also rumored to be the inspiration for Baskin Robbins 31 Flavors.

Before Baskin Robbins existed, Henry created and hand-churned 31 unique flavors of luscious ice cream. He made them, and chocolate Easter bunnies, in his laboratory, the dimly lit cement basement below the restaurant.

Henry was an ice cream artist. Picasso could have painted Guernica with strokes of Henry's Rotterburg Red Strawberry, Markdorf Orange Mango, Berlin Black Licorice, and Gluckstadt Green Pistachio.

He knew the secrets of coaxing out the maximum vanilla flavor in Von Hammerschmidt's Homestyle Vanilla, the deepest cocoa notes in Dresden Dark Chocolate, the smoothest caramel flavors in Burgdorf Butterscotch Swirl.

Customers rarely complained about his new flavors. But when they did, Henry ripped their bowls of uneaten ice cream off the lunch counter and stormed off, spewing German cuss words.

Who could blame them?

Trebbin Tooty Fruity sounded like fruit chunks blown out of a German tuba. Coswig Cotton Candy may have been the first ice cream that stuck to your face. Mulhausen Mustard Marshmallow tasted like s'mores revolting enough to scatter a campfire circle of small German children.

I worked behind the marble-topped lunch counter at Beier's. A line of red leather stools perched on chrome posts welcomed locals and out-of-towners. Dark oak booths created cozy dining nooks for couples, families, and business colleagues. Whether breakfast, lunch, or dinner, no meal ended without a scoop of one or more of Henry's 31 flavors.

Mr. Moppel managed the menu and business. He greeted

his guests with a fun-loving twinkle in his eye. He knew almost every customer on a first-name basis and proudly spoke only one language, *New Yawk*.

"Lou, regula table and what'll it be—cawfee ooah Scotch?"

"Jack and Lois, how's Bonnie? Did she figya out da loong division yet? I could use some accountin' help myself, but I'm goin' broke runnin' dis joint. Nah, just kiddin'! I almost had ya, though, d'int I?"

"Chuck and Eddie, yous guys look younga every day. Grab ya seats at the counta and don't die on me and spoil da atmospheah!" Chuck and Eddie were in their eighties and always dressed in their rumpled dark suits, clip-on bow ties, and age-worn fedoras, a tradition they would never abandon, even in their open casket viewings later that year.

Mr. Moppel's sleepy eye always drifted left. So I leaned in that direction whenever he spoke to me. "Phil, didya see dat new movie *I Love You, Alice B. Toklas*? Just saw it last night at the Floral Theata. Dey laughed deir asses off when dey ate doze mari-ja-wanna brownies. I wanna try somma dat mari-ja-wanna. Know way-ah I could get some?"

Mr. M. asked me that in the kitchen while his hippie son, Mike, stoned out of his mind, broiled steaks, flipped burgers, and filled French fry baskets a few feet away.

Mike probably had a big stash of weed right under his father's nose in the apartment they shared above the restaurant. But he didn't want his father to know. That bewildered me because anyone (except Mr. M.) could see that Mike's glazed red eyeballs, random comments understood only by himself, and cranked-up Deep Purple kitchen music were signs that he lived and cooked in a place called Mike's Weed World.

As a chef, he undoubtedly ate whatever satisfied his munchies but did everything possible to prevent his father from recognizing his stoned state while cooking about 300 meals a night on a hot stove coated in flammable grease.

That left me to fulfill my boss's wish, but buying pot for him could backfire if he freaked out when he got high and blamed me. "I've heard of marijuana, Mr. Moppel, but nevva tried it and wouldn't know way-ah to buy it. It does sound like fun though. If ya find some, I'd be happy to try it witchya."

I wasn't lying. That late '60s pot thing was a mystery to me. My guess is, that moment of honesty built a bridge, a bond between me and Mr. Moppel. He began to trust me with more and bigger responsibilities.

I oversaw sandwich meat prep for Beier's famous thinly sliced turkey, ham, pastrami, and roast beef sandwiches on white, wheat, rye, or hard rolls. I put my fellow worker and school buddy, Georgie Giordano, in charge of the meat-slicing machine. The dangerous electric contraption featured a spinning circular blade and adjustable meat holder that the *slicerone* slid back and forth across the blade, producing paper-thin cuts of meat.

Georgie slid a hunk of roast beef through the blade and sliced off the tip of his thumb. Henry nonchalantly walked by and muttered, "*Dummes kind,*" or "dumb kid," a term he addressed us with daily as a sign of affection, as Nazis will do.

Mr. Moppel assigned me to be Henry's assistant in the basement, making chocolate bunnies for the Easter parade of shoppers about to descend on Beier's. I'd never fried an egg, no less made something as complicated as chocolate Easter bunnies.

I arrived at work two minutes late on my first day working with Henry. He met me at the front door, arms folded, stiff as a Wehrmacht statue. "Vehr av you bean? Za rabbits are vaiting. Eet ees time to open za molts. Follow me! Mach schnell!"

I walked at a fast clip behind Henry past the lunch counter, through the double kitchen doors where stoner Mike examined a fly on the wall, and down the steep back stairs into the basement.

Three fluorescent light fixtures swung from the hot water pipes attached to the low ceiling. Why the lights swung, I'll never know. My only explanation was that the lights were shaken by the negative energy streaming from Henry's pores. The swinging lights created a frightful scene of shifting shafts of light and shadow. This was Henry's chocolate chamber and my torture chamber.

Even the euphoric fragrance of boiling chocolate didn't overcome my mounting fear of being locked in the basement with a grumpy Nazi version of Willy Wonka.

Brilliant blue tongues of gas-burner flames licked the bottoms of large copper kettles in the corner of the chamber. I could hear the glub-glub of bubbling chocolate. Henry turned his back to me and gripped the neck of a wooden spoon approximately the size of a two-by-four used to frame a house. He stirred the chocolate in slow, sweeping circles. I could almost see his back and shoulder muscles writhing under his crisp white cook's jacket above his houndstooth chef's trousers.

Henry ordered me to stand by the large butcher block table in the center of the basement. When he finished stirring the kettles, he slowly turned and approached the butcher block bunny altar, where I nervously side-stepped back and forth from one foot to the other.

The light hanging above the table illuminated Henry's gaunt, pasty white face and tiny rat eyes. He pointed to the silvery metal Easter Bunny "molts" standing at attention at the end of the table. "Do you see zees?"

I thought, *What kind of question is that?* An entire army of rabbit molds stood at attention in front of me. A blind man couldn't miss seeing them.

I sarcastically replied, "Yes, sir, Mista Henry, sir."

"Don't get shmart vit me, Mister Vize Guy," Henry growled through clenched chocolate-stained teeth. "Vee are here to do za serious verk, and you joke vit me? You joke? Do you sink zat making za best chocolate rabbits in za verld ees a laughing matta? Eet is time to get to verk. I show you how to remove za rabbits from zair cages."

All of the molds contained hollow chocolate bunnies already prepared and refrigerated by Henry. Apparently, he didn't want me to observe and steal his secret recipe and process. He just wanted me to open the molds and release his rabbits from captivity.

Henry slid one of the rabbit molds to the center of the table. "First, you open za clasp on za back of za rabbit." Henry tapped the mold and popped the clasp open with a quick flick of his thumb.

Then he opened the two hinged halves of the mold and lifted out a perfect chocolate bunny. Upturned corners of the bunny's mouth formed a smile, an unexpected signature feature coming from an angry German who last smiled during the Nazi occupation of Paris.

The smiling bunny was sadly ironic considering that a small girl wearing a flowery spring Easter bonnet would soon bite off the hare's head.

Henry placed another mold between us on the table. "Now you try, ya?" It was not a request.

I began to age rapidly with early onset hand tremors. I put my trembling left hand around the mold, giving it the appearance of a very jittery rabbit. I tried desperately to flip open the clasp, but the rabbit kept hopping to and fro in my shaking right hand.

I somehow managed to pop open the mold. All of my shaking shattered the rabbit. It tumbled out onto the butcher block in bite-sized chocolate ears and body parts.

Henry gasped. He reached across the table and stuck his

pointer finger into my chest. "LOOK VHAT YOU AFF DONE! ZA RABBIT EES KAPUT! I ONLY SAY ZIS VUNCE—DON'T FORCE ZA MOLTS!"

Despite his shock and anger, he gave me one more chance to prove I could be a successful rabbitteer. "You vill do zis again. Fasta zis time—and no shaking! Today vee vill open za twelf duhsen rabbits. Vee vill nevva reach zis objectif going at za slow pace of za turtle! You must shprint like za hare!"

Henry pushed me too far. Nothing I did pleased him. He would not win this power struggle. I locked eyes with him across the table. Without looking down, I tapped and unclasped the mold and removed a perfect smiling bunny in one rapid, seamless maneuver.

Henry didn't react except for the subtle rise of one eyebrow, which I interpreted as the unspoken words, *Maybe za dumm kind can do zis.*

He swiveled about-face on his heels and returned to the copper kettles to make the day's last batch of chocolate.

I surveyed the job before me. Twenty-three molds to open. Another ten dozen in the walk-in cooler waited to be set free. I could do this. Possibly maybe.

I reached for the nearest mold and accidentally knocked it over. When I opened the two metal halves, the bunny came out in Humpty Dumpty pieces that could not be put back together again. If Henry saw my mistake, who knows what disaster might happen next? Fortunately, the kettles weren't large enough to boil an entire pimple-faced five-foot-eight teenager.

I looked around. Not a garbage can in sight to hide the remains of the Bunny Day. I concluded that I could only make the bunny parts disappear by eating them. I stuffed the entire pile of bunny bits into my mouth. Henry would never find them in my stomach. I hoped.

It's surprising how long it took to chew and swallow a six-inch-tall Easter Bunny. Lumps of chocolate became lodged in my molars, forcing me to slowly suck and pick them out before I could swallow them. The chocolate expanded in my mouth and transformed into a thick, viscous sludge that was impossible to swallow quickly. The goo formed a long rope not unlike one a spelunker might use to descend the throat of an underground cave.

The clock ticked down. I had to eat the bunny and open more molds before Henry found out that I was single-handedly destroying his battalion of bunnies.

I opened another mold, this time with extra care. An avalanche of chunks toppled out carrying miniature slabs of chocolate shale. With no other option, I stuffed bunny number two in my mouth—also occupied by the torso of bunny number one.

How long could I keep up this rabbit charade? I had 20 molds to go on the table and enough stomach space remaining to handle three more at most. That's exactly the number of bunnies I broke during the next three tries.

The rabbits were behind by a score of 0 to 5, and we were only 10 minutes into the first quarter.

It occurred to me that if I continued to consume shattered rabbits, I might overdose on chocolate and keel over, alone with Henry in the basement of Beier's Restaurant.

Imagine my surprise when Henry the Nazi, of all people, saved my life. He didn't do anything heroic, like give me the Heimlich Maneuver to dislodge a chocolatey rabbit's foot from my windpipe.

Henry turned around from his boiling kettles. When he caught me pounding bunny parts into my mouth, he yelled, "Leef now! Out wit you! How many times do I haf to tell you? DON'T FORCE ZA MOLTS!"

MOON LANDING AT
MOTEL SEX

"That's one small step for man, one giant leap for mankind."
- Neil Armstrong, Moon Landing

In July 1969, Neil Armstrong, Buzz Aldrin, and Michael Collins hurtled 240,000 miles through space to the moon. Hundreds of millions of earthlings sat on the edge of their seats as a television camera attached to the lunar module beamed images of Armstrong's first step onto the barren lunar surface. I didn't *see* the moon landing on the nearby black-and-white Zenith TV, but I *heard* Armstrong's first words. When The Eagle landed, my eyes were closed in the heat of a marathon make-out session on the couch with summer girlfriend, Debbie Wheeler. Neil didn't specifically say, "Phil, I forgive you for missing the moon landing. Take one small make-out step for man and one giant leap for man and womankind." But it was definitely implied.

Debbie and I were babysitters at a seaside motel in the Hamptons on Long Island. We watched kids when their parents, usually on holiday from New York City, went out for a romantic evening dinner. Little Eddie slept in the bedroom during the moon landing while Debbie and I kissed on the couch until we rubbed our lips raw.

Like our inattention to the TV broadcast, we failed to hear Eddie's parents return to the motel room until it was too late. Mr. and Mrs. Liebowitz took one small step toward us and one giant leap for infuriated parents. They didn't want to wake Eddie and yelled at us in a diatribe of screaming whispers.

"HOW DARE YOU?!!! WE LEAVE YOU FOR A FEW HOURS TO TAKE CARE OF OUR SON, AND LOOK AT THIS! LOOK! YOU SHOULD BE ASHAMED OF YOURSELVES! AND DON'T THINK FOR A MINUTE THAT WE WON'T REPORT YOU TO THE MANAGER. YOU'RE BOTH IN BIG TROUBLE. BIG! GET OUT!"

My first thought was, *I guess getting paid is out of the question.* For a brief moment, I also considered informing them that Neil Armstrong himself not only gave us permission to make out on the couch, but he encouraged it.

The next day, the motel owner, Mr. Marlin, relieved us of babysitting duties. He re-assigned Debbie to the chambermaids and me to lifeguard duties. I lounged by the pool five days a week, bronzed in the sun, swam, practiced tricks off the diving board, and chatted with guests who worked in interesting jobs on Wall Street, on Madison Avenue, and for New York's Gambino mafia family.

After a month, I perfected a diving board trick that I dubbed "The Backward Head Dive." It featured a headstand, push-off, and heels-over-head backward flip feet-first into the pool.

On a sweltering Saturday afternoon, I performed my trick

dive for the crowd of poolside guests. I announced through the bullhorn, "Ladies and gentlemen, please direct yaw attention to the divin' board where I will pafawm a death-defyin' trick nevva befaw attempted. Be faw-wawned; this amazin' feat may not be appropriate faw children." Every kid raced to the edge of the pool.

The crowd hushed. I walked to the end of the board, rotated into the downward headstand position, and launched myself into the air. Unlike previous successful attempts, I dropped straight down, hit my head on the board, and collapsed into the deep end.

Later that day, a guest told me, "You should have seen it! When you fell into the pool, everybody cheered. I thought, this kid has some guts to hit his head like that on purpose. What a trick!"

The head bang knocked me out cold. As I slowly sank face-down toward the bottom of the pool, a hairy-chested mafia guy sporting a gold chain necklace dove in to save me, the *alleged* lifeguard.

You haven't experienced the full breath of life until you almost drown, only to be revived with mouth-to-mouth resuscitation performed by a hitman.

———

"The Backward Head Dive" would not be my last lifeguard blunder. Motel staff celebrated the final weekend of the summer season with an event called "Willy's Day," named after the owner, William Marlin.

On Willy's Day, maintenance guys, groundskeepers, boat dock boys, and lifeguards carried chambermaids to the pool and jumped in.

That summer, I befriended a hysterically funny Black

chambermaid, Sunny. Whenever I stopped by a room that Sunny tidied up, she serenaded me with ridiculous parodies of pop songs like Janis Joplin's "Take Another Piece of My Cart," Bob Dylan's "Lay Lady Lay Across My Big Pull-Out Sofa Bed," and The Beatles little-known "Something in The Way He Lifeguards."

Sunny oozed sunny, sassy personality. We kissed one time and might have been a thing, except interracial couples were still shunned in 1969, and neither of us wanted to put the other in danger. Plus, Debbie and I were a thing. If she suspected that Sunny and I were also a thing, some bad thing would happen.

Debbie was a Wheeler, not a Gambino, but she knew a thing or two about taking out her enemies or at least scaring the hell out of them. In Sunny's case, that might have involved changing a bed where Debbie cleverly hid a decapitated seagull head under the sheets.

Debbie kissed like a Siren but could fight like a Cyclops, a defensive skill she learned while growing up with her four rowdy brothers. I saw her in action at a family barbecue.

Her oldest brother, Bruce, squirted a squeeze bottle of mustard on her head. She locked him in a pro wrestler sleeper hold around the neck, followed by a full body slam onto the brick patio. Her last move was a Debbie classic. She grabbed the squeeze bottle and force-fed mustard into the muffled misery of Bruce's condiment-guzzling mouth.

Pissing off Debbie could have been a fatal mistake for me. Sunny and I agreed to just be friends. Debbie and I stayed monogamous through our summer of body slams and sleeper holds of a more pleasant kind.

Willy's Day arrived. I ran from room to room, searching for Sunny. When I finally found her, she held up her hands, palms facing me in a "back off" pose. "Now listen to me, Philodendron, there ain't no way you're picking me up and throwing me in that pool!"

In my clueless man-child ADHD brain, I heard, *Phil, please hold me in your arms and take me for a swim.*

I swept Sunny off her feet, kicking and screaming, and carried her across the lawn to the pool. My knucklehead failed to recognize that screams, like Henry's ice cream, came in lots of different flavors. There's the erotic love-making scream, the side-splitting laughing scream, the painful scream when you lose someone you love, and the terrified scream of Sunny, the formerly sunny chambermaid.

If only she had filled me in. It's a poor excuse, but I didn't know she couldn't swim. I stepped off the deep end with Sunny in my arms.

She panicked, pulled my hair with both of her hands and pushed me under the water to prop herself up. Once again, I found myself drowning in the pool. And, this time, neither Neil Armstrong nor a member of the Gambino family was coming to rescue me.

At the last second, before I inhaled a lung full of chlorinated pool water, my training kicked in (obtained by reading a 12-page *How to Be a Lifeguard* pamphlet from the health section in the library). I tugged Sunny under the water to distract her and swam her to the side of the pool. She grabbed ahold of the ladder, gasping for air. She was madder than a drowning Diana Ross singing "Stop in the Name of Hate."

"Look what you did, you fool! I never learned swimmin'! You damn near killed me!"

"I'm sorry, Sunny. Oh Gawd, I'm really sorry. I wouldn'ta done it if I knew ya cou'nt swim. Let's get ya outta the pool." She didn't speak to me for the rest of the afternoon.

The next day was our last workday of the summer season. I had to patch things up with Sunny before we went our separate ways. I slowly approached a room she was cleaning and stood in the open doorway holding a bouquet of summer wildflowers

I'd picked. Sunny's distressed expression softened a bit when I apologized by serenading her with a Motown song parody.

"Sunny, you shined and I really caused you pain
  Soon we'll be gone
  Please forgive this jerk
  Let's be friends, and make it work
  Sunny one so true, I love you-oo."

Sunny perched her hands on her hips and struck an arms-akimbo power pose. "I accept your apology, Philodendron. But don't take me swimmin' again, or next time *you* ain't gonna shine. *You* gonna drown and drown good."

The following summer, Mr. Marlin hired me as the day camp counselor. I was surprised that he allowed me to work with kids again after the make-out incident with Debbie in little Eddie's hotel room.

He either forgot about it or simply wasn't concerned because Debbie took another summer job at the local Carvel ice cream stand, far out of lip's reach.

That summer, the motel hosted a record number of families with little squirts. I could manage six of them playing croquet, shuffleboard, hopscotch, and whatever else I dreamed up to keep them entertained and away from their parents. But a seventh ankle-biter added a level of chaos on par with the storming of the Bastille. I begged Mr. Marlin to hire a second counselor before I lost what was left of my rapidly deteriorating mind.

Enter Carol—a cool, calm, cute blonde-haired college

student. We became instant friends. On the first day, she joined me in leading "Ring-Around-The-Rosie," a cheery nursery rhyme for children about death by Black Plague.

Carol and I and a dozen spoiled rug rats held hands and danced in a circle.

We gleefully sang about the red rings that ulcerated the skin of plague victims, not to mention the pockets full of Posies used to mask the foul odor of rotting flesh. When we reached the uplifting "ashes to ashes" crescendo about burning mountains of dead bodies, we all fell down laughing. Who wouldn't?

Imagine my surprise when little Eddie showed up a few days later to join us on a field trip to the movies. His mother shot me the stink eye, "No shenanigans like last year, buster."

She handed a ten-dollar bill to Carol and smiled. "I know *you'll* take good care of my Eddie. Here's five dollars for his movie ticket and popcorn and five dollars for you." She bribed Carol and belittled me in one fell swoop.

It became obvious to me that Eddie's mother might be the leader of a cult dedicated to torturing puppies. He was a great kid despite having been raised by, well, let's just call her Cruella the Puppy Torturess.

Eddie took a shine to me as if we were big and little brothers. He was small for seven years old and barely three feet tall. He could have been mistaken for a pint-sized comedian. Eddie's head resembled a princess cut diamond—flat on top with a triangular jawline that descended to the tip of a chin sharp enough to skewer a small house pet. Eddie's diamond head was oversized in proportion to his munchkin body, the visual effect being an upside-down pyramid of cheddar cheese balanced on a toothpick.

No one could ignore Eddie (but God knows, they tried). His loud, high-pitched voice could easily go on record as the only sound to fall within the hearing range of the deaf.

"HI, PHIL! WHAT MOVIE ARE WE GOING TO SEE? I'VE

BEEN TO THE MOVIES SIX TIMES, AND I'M ONLY SEVEN! THIS WILL BE MY SEVENTH TIME TO SEE A MOVIE. THAT'S RIGHT! SEVEN MOVIES IN SEVEN YEARS! DO YOU THINK THAT MEANS I'LL HAVE TO WAIT ANOTHER YEAR TO SEE MY EIGHTH MOVIE WHEN I'M EIGHT?"

The kid cracked me up. He jabbered during the whole drive to the theater in the hotel's station wagon. Eddie faced backward in the third bench seat and commented on everything that caught his attention out the rear window.

"LOOK EVERYBODY! THAT LADY DRIVING BEHIND US IS PICKIN' HER NOSE!"

"WHO WANTS TO COUNT TELEPHONE POLES WITH ME? ONE, TWO, THREE...SIXTY-THREE, SIXTY-FOUR, SIXTY- FIVE...ONE HUNDRED AND ELEVEN, ONE HUNDRED AND..."

"HEY, WE JUST DROVE PAST A SKUNK SLEEPING IN THE MIDDLE OF THE ROAD WITH HIS TONGUE STICKING OUT. CAN WE GO BACK AND WAKE HIM UP SO HE DOESN'T GET RUN OVER?"

The middle-aged Italian diva in the theater's ticket booth looked as if selling tickets was a sideline while she pursued her big acting break in the movie business. After all, loads of celebrities vacationed in the Hamptons. Sooner or later, a producer, director, or casting agent would recognize her striking resemblance to a Sophia Loren of the future (meaning, what Sophia might look like in 10 or 20 years with the same number of added pounds).

"How many tickets, signore?" she asked in a smoky two-pack-a-day Romanesque accent.

"Nine, please," I answered.

"*Si, nove.* And how many *bambini*?"

Carol interjected, "*Sette.*" She had learned conversational Italian in preparation for studying abroad in Florence in the coming semester.

"*Fantastico*! Your Italiano is *molto bene*," Sophia remarked, pleased to converse in her native tongue with Carol, the fair-skinned non-Italian daughter of Norwegian immigrants.

We shuffled the kids into the lobby and picked up Cokes, buttered popcorn, and boxes of Good & Plenty, Dots, and Sugar Babies at the concession stand.

The Art Deco theater was surprisingly crowded for a Tuesday matinee. We found nine seats together in the center section. Little Eddie climbed up onto the purple velour seat beside me. A big, burly guy sitting in front of Eddie blocked his view.

"HEY, PHIL. I CAN'T SEE THE SCREEN. CAN YOU ASK THE BIG MAN IN FRONT OF ME TO MOVE?"

The man rustled in his seat, annoyed. I whispered to Eddie, "Shhh. Be polite and I'll let ya sit on my lap."

Eddie climbed over the armrest between us and pointed at the burly guy's wife seated in front of us. "THAT'S MUCH BETTER, PHIL! I CAN EVEN SEE OVER THIS LADY'S BIG HEAD. WANT SOME POPCORN?"

Then he turned to the rest of the kids and called out, "WHO'S HOGGIN' THE SUGAR BABIES? PASS 'EM DOWN! I BET THIS BIG LADY WANTS SOME!"

I again asked Eddie to quiet down and explained that it wasn't polite to shout in a theater where the audience wanted to watch the movie without distractions. "OK, PHIL! WHATEVER YOU SAY!" Those were Eddie's last words until his tour de force outburst when the movie started.

I picked *They Call Me Mister Tibbs* because it was the only afternoon matinee within an hour's drive of the hotel. I knew nothing about the film other than it starred Sidney Poitier.

I figured *Mister Tibbs* would be suitable for children, probably along the lines of other wholesome family movies he starred in, such as *Lilies of the Field*. This was not one of those films.

Seven small children under my care were about to witness a gritty detective story involving the murder of a prostitute, a profession about 2,000 years older than Eddie.

The theater lights faded. I realized my mistake from the first scene. As the opening credits rolled, naked silhouettes of gyrating pole dancers filled the screen. The theater roared when they heard Eddie's high-pitched voice sail above the steamy alto sax soundtrack.

"LOOK, PHIL! BOOBIES!"

I turned to Carol.

"Do ya think we should leave?"

"*Aspettiamo e vediamo.*"

"What?"

"Let's wait and see."

We stayed for the rest of the movie, which featured several sex scenes but no visible private parts. Nevertheless, I worried that little Eddie would exuberantly brief his mother, Cruella, about the boobies he saw while bouncing on my lap in a dark theater.

Last summer, I became known as the motel's oversexed babysitter and drowned lifeguard. This year, I managed to expand my misfit reputation to "suspected child predator posing as a trusted camp counselor."

Shortly after we drove back to the motel, Mister Marlin found out about *Mister Tibbs*. Cruella warned him to keep me away from children. I finished out the season running the laundry room, the overlord of all things linen and cotton.

Carol felt guilty that I took the fall for the movie fiasco. She stopped by the laundry room every day to see me. Before she left for Italy, she came to say goodbye and brought me a gift.

Eddie appeared behind her, a dwarf standing in the doorway between two industrial-size washing machines. "*ARRIVEDERCI, FILIPPO! GRAZIE PER ESSERE MIO AMICO!*"

His Italian tutor, Carol, interpreted. "Thank you, Phil, for being my friend!"

And in that one unadulterated moment of friendship and innocence, Eddie washed away my summer of bitterness like a heavy laundry load rinsed clean of impurities.

❧ 21 ❧
BORN TO BE GROUNDED

"Ward, I think you were a little hard on Beaver tonight."
- Mrs. Cleaver

G rowing up in the 1960s was a blend of *Leave It to Beaver* and *Leave It to Griever*. Bad things happened. In threes. We were glued to our TV sets watching the shocking back-to-back-to-back assassinations of John F. Kennedy, Robert Kennedy, and Martin Luther King. Rock stars Jim Morrison, Janis Joplin, and Jimi Hendrix all overdosed and died within 10 months. Compared to them, my three bad things at the age of 15 weren't so bad. Although, death would have shortened my father's sentence, "You're grounded—until hell freezes over."

#1 Bad Thing

The first incident occurred when my parents drove off on a weekend trip and left Richie and me at home alone. Having the house to ourselves without adult supervision, compounded by my ADHD impulsiveness, created all sorts of opportunities to get into trouble. I narrowed those options down to a Friday overnight party in the basement with a bunch of buddies. We did what any red-blooded American teenagers would do for fun—anything forbidden by our parents.

The ten of us emptied our pockets and tossed $27.13 in bills and coins into a bowl and gave the money to Peter, the drinking-age brother and alcohol deliveryman of friend Billy Ferrantino. Peter returned to the house with two cases of dirt-cheap Ballentine beer and a jumbo-sized bottle of Ancient Age whiskey large enough to give a raging hangover to the entire Eastern seaboard.

Half of us sat around the game table playing penny poker, swearing like sailors, and smoking cigars. The other half played Eight Ball on our small foldable pool table with white plastic pockets and side bumpers so rock-hard they could foil a bank shot by Minnesota Fats himself.

The noise level rose in direct proportion to the amount of alcohol consumed. A salty-snack food fight broke out, covering the floor in a layer of pulverized potato chips, pretzels, and peanuts.

At one point, I looked over at my little Italian buddy, Gino Gralisi, hunched over as he regurgitated his dinner of clam linguini on my mother's prized braided oval rug, now resembling a steaming seafood platter from a minus-four-stars Little Italy cafe.

Another buddy, Biff Bukoski, announced, "I'll be right back. I have to run an errand." About an hour later, I realized Biff hadn't returned. Or did he?

Biff was nearly blind and wore black glasses with lenses as thick as Coke bottles. The lenses enlarged his eyes, producing the effect of a talking frog. His errand could end badly, wandering around outside in the dark with the visual acuity of a drunken lily pad hopper.

I searched the house and found Biff passed out in the

second-floor bathroom, his face as white as a vampire blood donor. He ran an errand, all right. Biff returned with an official Floral Park police badge pinned to his shirt pocket. How he procured the badge from a cop in our town remained a mystery, even to Biff.

I ran down to the basement to get help before he croaked. Three of us dragged Biff into the shower, fully clothed. A half-hour cold shower sobered him up a bit.

We stripped off his soaking wet clothes, dressed him in a pair of my flannel pajamas, and tucked him into bed. He refused to remove his glasses, slurring something about how he needed them to see a dream about Jeanie Dabrowski, the hottest girl in school, also cut from Polish cloth.

I realized that the party had crossed a line somewhere between a buddy night and the bombing of Hiroshima. I had to get everybody out of the house for a breather, for time to settle down. We stepped out into the cold winter night and discussed our options in the driveway.

Three guys could barely walk. Four laughed so loudly at anything, funny or not (why would anyone think the word "horseshoe" was hysterically funny?) that I became concerned they'd wake up the neighbors, who'd call the cops. Then we'd really be in trouble, especially if the cop who showed up wasn't wearing a police badge and asked if we had a friend who looked like a frog.

That left an obvious though risky choice. I grabbed the car keys to our Chrysler New Yorker family station wagon for a drive to the Bellerose Diner to get some alcohol-absorbing breakfast in our bellies. We faced two minor obstacles. None of us had a driver's license. And reversing out of the garage down the long, narrow driveway between our house and the neighbor's house would be tricky, kind of like backing up a battleship through a Venetian canal.

All nine of us, minus sex-dream Biff and my brother, packed into the station wagon like beer-boiled sardines. Unlike an actual trained driver with a license, I used two feet to operate the brake and accelerator pedals.

The car jerked in reverse as I continuously stepped on the gas and slammed on the brake. I looked in the side-view and rear-view mirrors, watching my brother, illuminated in the red taillights, furiously waving directions with flailing arms.

With his reluctant help, I somehow managed to back out of the driveway and into the street without hitting the house at H.M.S. Chrysler ramming speed.

The jerky ride continued as we lurched our way to the diner at two o'clock in the morning through dimly lit streets, stop signs, and red lights. The silvery bread-loaf outline of the diner came into view, glowing like Mecca beckoning crowds of starving late-night pilgrims. We pulled into the only space left in the parking lot. We weren't the only tipsy pilgrims in need of a sobering ham and cheese omelet—just the youngest.

The hostess, wearing a pale blue uniform and hair net, greeted us with a forced smile perfected over years of late-shift experience. Her body language delivered the unspoken message, *Please leave, you underage nitwits*. But to avoid any misunderstanding, she told us, "A table should free up soon, boys. Shouldn't be more than, oh, 90 minutes."

We filed out the door. Backing out of the long bowling alley that was my driveway instilled in me a false sense of driver confidence. Instead of backing straight out of the parking spot, I turned the wheel and floored it.

The right front bumper shredded the side of the car next to us from the front door to the rear fender panel. I panicked, turned off the headlights, and sped out of the lot as fast as I could to avoid being seen by any witnesses.

In a matter of seconds, my life had gone south from a law-abiding teenager to a hit-and-run driver speeding toward a juvenile jail sentence.

When we arrived home, I hid the alcohol and led the clean-up. That included wiping Gino's pasta pile off the braided rug and flipping the rug over to hide the stain from my parents. It never occurred to me that mothers notice things like re-arranged home décor.

Mom and Dad came home late Sunday afternoon. I walked on eggshells and nervously waited for them to find a mess I'd overlooked or wonder why the air smelled like day-old clam linguini. I worried that one of my friend's parents would call to complain that, "My boy came home from your house and almost died from alcohol poisoning." Worse yet, what if the owner of the car I wrecked called my father and informed him that I had smashed his car and drove away from the scene of the crime?

None of those bad imaginings happened that Sunday. But I soon discovered the meaning of the phrase "wait for it."

When I came home from school Monday afternoon, our olive-green rotary wall phone rang in the kitchen.

A man asked, "Hello. Is this Philip Caragol?"

"Yeah, dis is Phil."

"Phil, my name is Tom Doolittle. You hit my car Friday night in the parking lot at the Bellerose Diner."

"Dat's impossible, Mista Doolittle. I don't *own* a cahh oah even *have* a drive-uh's license."

"That's unfortunate, Phil. I have to tell you that I know your father and someone at the diner recognized his car and you behind the wheel. Here's what I propose. The body shop says they can repair the damages for $500. We can keep this between us if you pay me the $500 in cash by this Friday. Otherwise, I'll have no choice but to get your father involved, and I think that's something you may want to avoid."

"*Yes, I do, sir.* Thank you. May I have yaw numbba?"

I hung up the phone. Beads of sweat trickled down my fore-head. That only left four days to get my hands on $500. I called every friend who came to the party. "He-ah's the deal. I'm screwed if I don't come up with the money. Can ya help me out? I need $500 by Friday. Got any cash layin' around? Safety deposit box? Paycheck comin' in? Anybody owe ya who hasn't paid up yet? Wanna buy nine bottles of Ballentine and four shots of Ancient Age?"

Turns out that 15-year-olds are not the best source of fund-ing. Their donations amounted to $51.87 or $448.13 short. It's not that they weren't good friends. It's that they were good friends whose financial assets could only be counted in pennies, nickels, dimes, and quarters.

That left me facing a worst-case scenario.

When my dad arrived home from his law office Thursday night, I poured him a glass of scotch on the rocks and asked if I could talk to him in the living room. He looked pleased that I asked him to have a father-son talk. He had no idea what was coming. "That sounds great, my boy. Let me change and I'll be right down."

Dad returned in his favorite light-yellow chamois shirt and khaki pants. He sat down in the upholstered high-backed chair next to the fireplace. I sat directly opposite him on the loveseat, the coffee table between being the only thing that separated us. It would come in handy as a defensive obstacle in case he tried to lunge across the divide to strangle me.

"So, what's on your mind, Flip?" That's the pet name Dad used when he was in an affectionate, fatherly mood.

"Well, Dad. I dunno how to tell ya this. So I'll just cut to the chase." Anxiety lines crept across his forehead. "I had a pahdee last Friday when you and Mom were gone." He stroked the crown of his bald head from front to back. "I drove the cahh and got in an accident at the Bellerose Diner." He set down his glass of scotch.

"You what?"

"I know. I did a stupid ting, Dad. I shoulda nevva gotten in the cahh. I'm sorry. Nobody was hurt. Except for the guy's cahh I hit in the pahkin' lot."

"You hit somebody? Do you realize how much trouble you could be in? You admitted it right away, didn't you?"

"No. I got scayed and drove awff."

"You what?"

"I panicked and drove awff. But I tawked over the phone when I got home today to a Mista Doolittle who owns the cahh."

"Jim Doolittle?"

"That's him."

"You wrecked my client's car and ran off?"

"I'm sorry, Dad. He said he knows ya and I need to give him $500 to fix the cahh. I dunno what to do. I made a big mistake. I'm really sorry!"

Dad looked away from me, picked up his scotch glass from the coffee table, and swirled the melting ice cubes in circles around the rim. "Go to your room. We'll talk about this later."

That night, he came into my bedroom. "I talked to Jim Doolittle. He's one of my best clients. You owe me $500 in chores. You're grounded. No friends over. No after-school activities. No TV."

"OK, Dad. I deserve it. I messed up and I'll make it right. By the way, how lawng am I grounded?"

"Until you pay back the $500, or hell freezes over. Whichever comes first."

#2 Bad Thing

Hell had not yet frozen over. But after two months of grounding and $300 left in chores to complete, the ice had thawed a bit.

On occasion, Dad would grant me a temporary reprieve. A

date with a girl here. An after-school club meeting there. I toed the line carefully, always asking for small freedoms. That is until a local concert was announced for my favorite rock band, Jethro Tull, and its gifted lead singer, songwriter, and flutist, Ian Anderson.

I might never again have had the chance to see Jethro Tull. Their combination of classical music training and heavy rock riffs could not be matched. They were a once-in-a-lifetime band. I would regret it for the rest of my life if I missed the show.

"Dad, I know dis is a big fayva to ask, but can I go see my favorite band play next Saturday? I've done everything you've asked. It would mean a lot to me, and I promise not to get outta line."

In retrospect, I wish I hadn't offered a 100% ironclad guarantee.

After a long pause, he said, "All right, Phil. You can go on one condition. You have to be home by 11 at the latest." I couldn't believe it. My best friend, Al, and I were going to see Jethro Tull on the U.S. tour of their new album *Aqualung*.

Al picked me up in his white Ford Galaxy sedan decked out with red and white striped leather seats, chrome dashboard, tail fins, and a monster 442 HP engine. On the way to the concert, we drank our favorite vile cocktail—plastic cups filled with equal parts Miller High Life and Boons Farm apple wine. The combination was only slightly more refreshing than a cup of battery acid.

When we arrived at the concert hall, I slipped the half-empty bottle of Boons Farm into the back of my jeans to sneak it into the concert. To reach the entry gate from the parking lot, we had to cross over a grassy knoll, slick with sprinkler dew.

When I walked down the knoll, both feet slipped out from under me. My legs flew up in the air and I crashed flat on my back. I heard the bottle pop in my pants as it exploded into shards of razor-sharp glass.

I stood up. Pieces of dark green glass made a tinkling sound as they toppled down my legs and out of my jeans onto the grass. Hippies standing in the entrance line pointed at me and laughed—until they saw me reach into the back of my pants and hold up my hand dripping with blood.

Al grabbed my arm and we hobbled to the ticket taker at the gate. He called a security guard who quickly escorted us to the nearest men's room inside the concert hall. I stood in front of the mirror mounted over the double sinks. He said, "Drop your pants." I did. And along with it, his jaw dropped. "You better get to a hospital."

Al ran several red lights on the way to Long Beach Hospital. When we arrived at the ER, the desk nurse informed me that I would have to ask my parent's permission before a doctor would see me. *De-ah Gawd*, I prayed. *Please let it be my mutha who ansuhs the phone.*"

God came through. My sweet mom authorized the medical attention. She told me to come home right after I left the ER. A nurse whisked me and Al away to an examination room.

I laid face down on the gurney while the doctor picked slivers of glass out of my posterior. Al watched. Blood drained out of his face like the red fluid receding in a thermometer gauge.

Thirty-six stitches later, I was good to go and asked the doctor, "Is they-ah anything I should know about? Can I sit in a chay-ah? Wawk around?" I took his reply as permission to drive back to the concert. "You just had 36 stitches, son. You can do whatever you want and nothing's going to rip them out."

The combination of blood and alcohol rendered Al unable to drive. So I drove (this time with one foot on the pedals instead of two). We entered the hall at the perfect moment.

The warm-up act, Edgar Winter, had wrapped up. We

arrived when Jethro Tull walked out onstage. Ian Anderson's signature standing-on-one-leg performance, with the other leg kicking rooster-style, lit up the crowd. His breathy flute filled the hall with their top single, "Locomotive Breath."

When the song ended, Al had disappeared just like Biff at the Friday night party. I looked all over the auditorium and finally found him slumped over on a toilet seat in the men's room, drunk, and sick as a dog.

I dragged him out to the car, plopped him in the back seat, and drove home to become the lucky winner of a second butt-kicking.

When I pulled into the driveway, the Galaxy's clock hands read 1:15, more than five hours after I promised my mom I'd be home from the ER, and more than two hours after the curfew time set by my dad. This was bad. Who knows how long my grounding would last if my parents caught me coming home this late? But what if they didn't catch me? What if I just snuck into my room and they were none the wiser?

The only way to pull that off was to quietly enter through my second-story bedroom window. That presented a logistical challenge. I'd have to somehow climb the sheer wall of the house next to the driveway to reach my window.

Fortunately, we had an old 16-foot wooden ladder hanging from the fence in the backyard. Unfortunately, it weighed about 75 lbs., a heavy load for even two people to carry. Al was sound asleep in the back seat. I'd have to go it alone.

I lifted the ladder out of the S-hooks on the backyard fence, grasped the middle rungs, and staggered while carrying the huge ladder down the driveway.

In addition to the problem of raising the ladder, my brother Ted's black Oldsmobile was parked under my bedroom window. The space between his car and the wall left only a 12-inch gap to set the ladder. Determined to avoid a longer grounding period, I raised the ladder straight up between Ted's car and my window and started to climb.

According to physicists, "straight up" is not a recommended position for ladders and the idiots who climb them. Halfway up to my window, the ladder began to sway. I tried to balance it, teeter-tottering in midair like a skillful circus clown. But I faced the hard truth that I was all clown, no skill.

I plunged backward off the ladder and landed on my back on top of Ted's car, leaving a crater-like dent of my newly stitched-up rump in the roof.

I rolled down the windshield, off the hood, and landed spread-eagled on my back on the driveway. The kitchen lights blinked on. I stood up, walked to the door, and prayed, "*Sweet Jesus, let it be my mutha*."

For reasons unknown, some prayers are not answered. The door opened and my dad's fist shot out into my chest, knocking me to the ground.

"Go to bed. We'll talk in the morning." And the next morning, around five o'clock, Al revved his engine and screeched out of the driveway.

What a night we'd had. And what a well-deserved butt-kicking I got when the roar of Al's 442 HP engine woke up my dad. "Tell that damn fool to never come back to this house again! You're grounded for another month or until hell...."

#3 Bad Thing

Exactly how thick is a thick skull? Look no further than the undeveloped cranium of a boy who lives in denial about his poor choices, who learns nothing that might help to end his self-inflicted pain and start him on the road to adulthood. For the third time in six months, I missed the bus to the elusive village of Maturity.

The only bright spots in my extended grounding were rehearsals for my high school's upcoming performance of the

musical *Guys and Dolls*. My father granted me another temporary release to join the stage lighting crew five afternoons a
week for a month.

The show ran for two nights. That Friday and Saturday
happened to be the same nights my parents had planned a
weekend getaway to celebrate their 30th wedding anniversary.
Neither their weekend holiday nor my duties as a crew member
could be canceled. Once again, my parents allowed Richie and
me to stay home and fend for ourselves.

On his way out the door, Dad instructed us, "I don't want
any trouble, boys. Behave like men—do the right thing or else."

The right thing turned out to be the wrong choice. I offered
to host the cast and crew party at our house after the Saturday
night show. And what a show it was.

Guys and Dolls featured a big student cast of more than
thirty characters, singers, and dancers. Added to that were an
equal number of stagehands, lighting technicians, and set
builders, plus a twenty-piece student orchestra. My thick skull
failed to compute the math. A crowd of about one hundred
celebratory schoolmates was about to descend on our house,
all pumped up and ready to party after the show's epic ten-
minute standing ovation.

So many people rang the doorbell that it sounded like a
ding-dong orchestra of overly exuberant chime players. They
came in carrying six-packs of Coca-Cola and beer, bags of
chips, and a giant chocolate layer cake topped with *Guys and
Dolls* wax candle characters in various dancing poses.

The trouble started in the living room when Harry
Hotchkiss, who played the lead role of Sky Masterson, took the
last puff of his cigarette and stomped it out on my mother's
treasured gold wall-to-wall carpet.

Apparently, I wasn't the only guy in the room who missed
the bus to Maturity.

The embers of Harry's Marlboro left a telltale brownish

burn mark in the carpet, a small volcanic crater surrounded by fields of gold. There was no way to clean or patch it. So, I rearranged the furniture and covered the hole with the claw foot of the coffee table. I falsely hoped that my parents would appreciate my unique gift for interior decorating, first in the basement during #1 Bad Thing and now in the living room during #3 Bad Thing. If "Repeat Offender" was a doctorate program, I was well on my way to becoming *summa cum laude* of the class.

Most of the action happened in the basement. The party down there was in full swing. Couples dripping with sweat danced to The Doors long version of "Light My Fire." The skunk scent of pot permeated the air. So did a foreboding sense that something terrible was about to happen.

Guys and dolls occupied every bar stool, loveseat, and wall bench. Only one chair remained unoccupied—my father's favorite leather recliner.

More than a chair, the BarcaLounger was his oasis where he could escape to a mini home vacation, away from work and stress. Harming the recliner would be tantamount to taking away his right to happiness. That where he lounged, smoked his favorite cigars, and escaped into the TV worlds of Ben Cartwright in *Bonanza*, Fes Parker's *Daniel Boone*, *The Rifleman*, *Old Yeller,* and *Voyage to the Bottom of the Sea.*

I had to protect my father's sacred BarcaLounger at all costs. I scotch-taped a hand-printed sign on the chair. Large red letters commanded: "DO NOT SIT!" So far, everyone respected the warning. I stood guard behind the chair to make sure it came to no harm. Out of nowhere, I heard Stevie Gladsow's high-pitched Tarzan yell at the top of the basement stairs. "Ahhhh-ah-ah-ah-ahhhh-ah-ah-ah-ahhhh!"

He bounded down the stairs, planted both feet on the rug, and swan-dived from his imaginary jungle waterfall cliff into my father's beloved chair. The entire back of the lounger snapped off and collapsed on the floor in a limp heap.

I yelled, "Everybody out! Now!" And just like that, my order cast out the cast party. The One Hundred poured out of the front door, packed into their cars, and drove away. As they rolled down the street, I heard them sing the song that brought down the house earlier that night, "Sit Down, You're Rockin' The Boat." No kidding. Stevie Gladsow not only sat down, he swan-dived into the chair that would rock my boat for months or years.

I desperately needed a way to repair the BarcaLounger before my dad came home the next evening to watch Ben Cartwright teach his son, Little Joe, how to behave like a man.

The next morning, I pleaded with the two best handymen I knew—Richie and our friend who lived across the street, Holly. Between the two, they owned or had access to enough tools to fill the wing of a handyman museum.

They initiated triage on the lounge chair. We had six hours to finish the repairs before my parents walked in the door. Richie and Holly went to work.

Step 1: Identify problem. Holly flipped over the chair and used a utility knife to slice an unobtrusive opening in the leather upholstery. He examined the wooden joint that affixed the back of the chair to the seat and diagnosed the break. According to Holly, "The force of Stevie's body ripped the tempered-steel Phillips Head wood screws out of their 2-inch x 2-inch pine frame supports at a 45-degree angle." I took his word for it.

Step 2: Screw it. Richie retrieved new screws and wooden shims from the workshop. I held up the back of the chair while Holly held a flashlight. Richie removed the old screws and screwed the shims into the supports that held up the back of the seat. Theoretically, the back would now stand on its own.

We flipped over the chair into its full upright position. On the count of three, I released the back of the chair. It flopped over like a wet noodle.

Step 3: Dowels, screws and glue. Holly drilled a ½" hole through the connecting supports on both sides of the chair. He then inserted wooden dowels into the holes smeared with Super Glue that would theoretically set in two hours. We propped up the back of the chair and braced it with a couple of boards, similar to an easel-back holding up a wobbly picture frame.

Step 4: Re-test the chair. We removed the boards. The back held and temporarily stood upright, but ready to collapse with the slightest weight of its next reclining victim. We ran out of time. The repairs would have to suffice.

That evening, I waited for Dad to join me downstairs for the week's Sunday 8 o'clock episode of *Bonanza*. I heard his slippers swish down the dark green linoleum steps to the basement. He strolled in front of the color TV console in his brown plaid bathrobe on his way to the bar. "I'll be back in a minute, Flip." Dad poured a glass of scotch and returned, ready to settle in for an exciting hour of *Bonanza*.

Just as he was about to sit in the chair, I warned him, "Dad, stop! Don't sit down!"

"What? Why not?"

"I dunno how to tell ya this, so I'll just cut to the chase."

"Oh no. Not again."

"I had a cast pahdee last night. Somebody broke yaw chay-ah."

"What?"

"I can't tell ya who did it. I promised I wouldn't rat him out. I tried to fix it. But if ya sit back, ya could fawl backward and get hurt. I'll buy ya a new one. I sway-ah."

Unlike his response to the #1 and #2 bad things I'd done, my father took a slow sip of scotch and, in a gentle Ben Cartwright voice, uttered, "I see."

Years later, I realized that was his quiet way of telling me that I had made the right choice to protect him and was finally on my way to becoming a man.

❧ III ❧
THE WILD YEARS
1971-1975 A.D.H.D.

Hikin', smokin' and jokin' with college best friend and shaman, Jim, before he skysailed away from us forever.

ORANGE SUNSHINE ON MY
SHOULDERS

*"The brown acid that is circulating around us is not specifically too
good. It's suggested that you do stay away from that.
Of course, it's your own trip, so be my guest."*
- Woodstock Music Festival announcement

"Pay attention, class. We're going to watch an important movie about D-R-U-G-S." My stodgy old high school hygiene teacher, Mrs. Duncan, had an annoying habit of spelling touchy subjects. These also included S-E-X and D-E-F-E-C-A-T-E.

She pulled down the classroom's black window shades and flipped on the 16-mm movie projector. The anti-drug film, *Pit of Despair*, portrayed the tragic story of a clean-cut school track star's rapid decline from pot smoker to full-blown heroin addict. At the gut-wrenching climax, he rolled in agonizing withdrawals on a filthy mattress in an abandoned apartment building. Ironically, *Pit of Despair* plunged our hygiene room into such a pit of despair that several of us cut the next class to smoke a joint.

I never tried hard drugs in high school. That changed the

week I left home for college and moved into my freshman dorm in Boulder, the hippie capital of the Mountain West.

In 1971, almost no New Yorkers attended CU, the University of Colorado. We were a novelty, known mostly as uncouth tough guys in mafia movies and TV sitcoms.

By the time I unpacked the steamer trunk and settled into my dorm room, a line had formed outside the door. Kids from places like California and Kansas came to see the new attraction in room 200F who, rumor had it, grew up in Archie Bunker's Queens neighborhood portrayed in the ground-breaking TV sitcom, *All in the Family*.

My roommate, Mark, admitted one person at a time into our room. He'd spell out a prompt, Mrs. Duncan style. "Hey Phil, say W-A-L-K the D-O-G." I'd say, "Wauk the dawg." The dorm kids always busted up laughing.

My accent led to a small degree of popularity, which almost compensated for becoming a human freakshow.

"Hey Phil, what do you call a time when people get together and drink beer?"

"I dunno. A pahdee?"

"Phil, Phil, Phil. Tell us again. Where'd you grow up?"

"Why ya askin'? Ya already know. New Yawk."

And so on.

A long-haired California surfer dude and chemistry major down the hall, Tim Spangler, invited me and a few other guys to his room. He locked the door. We sat on the twin beds, facing each other.

Tim opened a large manila envelope and placed an orange ink blotter covered with smiling sunshine faces on the telephone spool table between the beds. It struck me as odd that Tim locked the door to give us smiley face stickers that appeared to be as harmful as safe S-E-X.

"Phil, you ever drop acid?" Tim asked.

"Shawah. Ah hell, akshally, I'm bullshittin' yuhs. Acid? Whasdat?" Guys rolled on the beds in stitches.

"It's magic. I brought enough for the whole floor. 100 tabs. Pure sunshine direct from Laguna Beach."

I figured, what's the worst that could happen? Any drug called Orange Sunshine had to be fun, kind of like having a giddy pot high while skipping hand-in-hand through a field of sunflowers.

We stuck out our tongues. Tim deposited a fingertip-size sunshine face in each of our mouths and smiled. "Gentlemen, we'll see you on the dark side of the moon."

Over the next eight hours, the familiar world I'd known my whole life cracked wide open. I entered a parallel dimension of heightened sight, sound, smell, touch, and high-speed mental processing. The portal to this new dimension was the dorm's second-floor hallway, filled with freshmen and freshwomen tripping their brains out.

The hall stretched to a distant point of near infinity (about 80 feet) where a gargantuan bright pink flamingo (girl wearing a red t-shirt) perched on a luminous white marble orb (water fountain) flapped its massive wings (waved her arms), and soared (jumped) over my head into the lush emerald green primordial jungle (onto the tile floor) thousands of feet (three feet) below, teeming with ravenous prehistoric reptilian beasts (hallucinating students eating trail mix).

At some point during my mind-expanding hallucinatory journey, I willed myself to fit in, began talking like a "Colo-rad-an," and lost my New York accent.

The following afternoon, I skipped across campus to my brother Richie's fraternity house to tell him about my first night in the dorm.

If not for him, I wouldn't have been in Colorado. My parents only let me apply to two colleges—Nassau Community near home on Long Island, where they could keep an eye on me, and CU, where they asked Richie to keep an eye on me. He was not thrilled to be my big-brother caretaker.

"Man, Richie. You wouldn't believe what happened last night."

"Oh, yeah?"

"Let me ask you this. Ever dropped acid?"

"Holy shit! Did you drop acid? What are you trying to do, get me in trouble with Mom and Dad?"

"Don't worry. They'll never know."

"They *would* if you OD'd. Acid's nothing to mess around with."

"No kidding. I think every synapse in my head fired at the same time. I saw stuff you wouldn't believe. Giant flamingos, wormholes, pigs playing banjos..."

"Just cool it, OK? We've got to get you out of the dorm. You can move in here with me and join the fraternity."

"Fraternity? Are you kidding me? No way I'm turning into a frat boy."

"Listen, little brother, just try it out. This isn't a frat boy frat. It's a great group of guys who just happen to live together in a fraternity."

Thanks to my newly expanded consciousness beaming with sunshine, I gave it a shot. In time, Sigma Delta would become a portal to yet another dimension, one in which a patchwork of quirky characters sought truth, love, honor—and occasionally, acid.

I joined the fraternity when fraternities weren't cool. Anti-establishment flower children flat-out rejected their parents' traditions, rules, and organizations. They grouped fraternities with elitist male chauvinist societies they detested, like the notorious Elks and Moose Club gangs.

Before the fall semester started, I hung out that summer with the remaining twelve members of the fraternity. We floated on inner tubes down Boulder Creek, hiked steep mountain trails, threw epic keg parties, and smoked weak pot in bean bag chairs with the Moody Blues, Zeppelin, and Cream cranked up on the stereo system.

I began to understand why these guys called themselves "brothers." They were tight like brothers but without the family baggage. I couldn't bear to see them become the next fatality in a mounting ash heap of fraternity closures. At an open house during fraternity Rush, I helped recruit more incoming freshmen. Our ragtag pledge class of misfits kept the fraternity alive:

- **Crusher:** Chicago wisecracker prone to fake wrestling matches; body hair akin to Sasquatch
- **Egore:** Photographic-memory ROTC fly boy and human beer receptacle
- **Tad:** House stand-up comic and Serbian teddy bear similar in size to Andrea the Giant
- **Wonder:** Son of a Methodist minister; explosives enthusiast named after subversive counter-culture comic book character Wonder Wart-Hog
- **Gook:** Way-out-there tall glass of free-thinking water, horror film aficionado, and rock guitar shredder who often performed dressed as Wolfman
- **Rock:** Playboy-in-training and future Navy pilot who broke the house record for most no-show dates in a single semester
- **Sluggo:** Stupidly happy hot dog skier, hang-glider, washboard player, trained outdoor survivalist, Eagle Scout, and hallucinogens expert resembling a frenetic elf
- **Howler:** Professorial, mild-mannered traditionalist often seen smoking a Sherlock Holmes pipe in a tweed jacket with suede elbow patches
- **Smitty:** Meticulous dresser with the cleanest room in the

house, including the closet, which he didn't come out of until after graduation.

Before we could be officially initiated into the fraternity, a nerdy upperclassman, Dick Whitweiser, gathered us together in the living room. He explained, "Next week is Hell Week. It's not as bad as it sounds. We'll ask you to do some things together to prove you're committed to the brotherhood. Bring everything you need to live here for a week. Any questions?"

Egore: "Yeah. Explain 'do things.'"

Dick: "Things like cleaning the house. You'll see."

Smitty: "Oh, I'm very good at cleaning. That doesn't sound like hell to me at all."

A booming voice snatched our attention. "Don't fool yourselves, boys! It'll *feel* like hell when you scrub every tile in the showers with a toothbrush!" The voice belonged to college senior and Hell Week Master, Danny O'Day.

When O'Day woke up on the first day of Hell Week, we served him a Bloody Mary in bed, a nauseating mixture of Heinz catsup and cheap vodka. He chugged the whole glass. "Not bad, boys. Now get to work!"

We headed to the second-floor bathroom, armed with toothbrushes and cylindrical cans of Ajax bleach cleanser. O'Day was right. Scrubbing shower tiles, sinks, and toilet bowls with a toothbrush was a hellishly boring experience, not unlike scouring the rust off a battleship with a sheet of number-two sandpaper.

When we finished cleaning the upstairs bathroom, O'Day led us down to the small half-bathroom under the basement stairs. All ten of us packed into the cramped water closet, which contained a toilet, sink, and vanity cabinet.

He pointed to a goldfish swimming in the toilet. "Boys, meet Big Gus. Gus is your beloved mascot for the rest of the week. You will treat him like a brother and keep him alive and healthy.

When any of you need to relieve yourselves, you must first ask for my permission. Once granted, you will come here as a group, fill the vanity basin with water, carefully scoop Gus out of the toilet bowl with this aquarium net, and safely place him in the basin."

Hell Master O'Day was far from finished. "Let me re-state, no one can relieve himself unless everyone's in the room with said brothers. Acknowledge and accept this critical assignment by repeating after me."

O'Day: "I am a scurb, sir!"

All: "I am a scurb, sir!"

O'Day: "A scurb is the lowest form of life!"

All: "A scurb is the lowest form of life!"

O'Day: "So low, in fact, to me, whale crap looks like a falling star!"

The sheer ridiculousness of a goldfish mascot named Big Gus and anything called a scurb pushed us over the edge. We laughed so hard our sides hurt—except for Tad, who thought O'Day said "Serb" and had insulted his people.

The next day's assignment was even more hilarious.

"It's lunchtime, boys," announced O'Day as he led us into the dining room. "Have a seat on opposite sides of the table. We have something special in store for your mutual nourishment." The words "mutual nourishment" raised all kinds of red flags. O'Day was diabolically creative.

The kitchen door swung open. Five upperclassmen carried plates of white navy beans and set them down in front of us on the long oak dining table. The beans swam in a lumpy grayish sauce of unknown origin, a sure sign that Big Gus would have plenty of company soon.

Crusher turned to O'Day. "So let me guess. You want us to eat this slop with our hands?" He corrected Crusher. "Hands? No, boys, we don't eat like animals here. We use utensils. Unfortunately, we ran out of utensils. You will have to feed each other with these." He reached under the table and pulled out a milk crate filled with lightbulbs.

Non-plussed, Tad peered across the table at Smitty and snickered, "Open wide. Through the lips and over the gums, look out stomach, here it comes." Tad used the lightbulb to shovel navy beans from the plate into Smitty's mouth. Gooey sauce dripped off Smitty's chin and splattered his neatly pressed Oxford button-down shirt.

The rest of us followed their lead. All five pairs of pledges fed each other across the table. I imagined that this might have been what a romantic Valentine's dinner looked like on an acid trip.

"Darling, may I have another bulb of beans?"

"Oh yes, dear, with or without lumpy sauce?"

Hell Week united us into a band of lifelong brothers. We didn't know it at the time, but O'Day helped us prepare for the real world after college. Those seven days taught us a lot about the value of teamwork, persistence, and hard work.

We faced every adversity together, including the premature death of Big Gus, who was tragically flushed out to sea.

❧ 23 ❧

ALASKA BITES

"Ain't no hick cop in this two-bit town gonna arrest me."
- Actor Steve McQueen, 1972, arrested for DUI
and reckless rental car racing in downtown
Anchorage, the week before our arrival.

S luggo's dad dropped us off by the side of Highway 101 in Sausalito with heavy backpacks and light wallets. We were hitchhiking to Alaska, the summer vacation destination of every mosquito on earth.

If it all worked out, my college buddy and I would spend the summer working at a fish cannery with college friends Bob and Laurie, who traveled to Anchorage ahead of us. Laurie grew up in the rugged gateway city to the Alaskan wilderness. She coaxed us to join them with a coin toss of sorts—jobs chopping the heads and tails off of King Salmon. At the stupendous pay rate of $25 an hour, we'd earn enough cash to cover a large portion of our college expenses and buy a hundred-gallon drum of Old Spice aftershave to cover up the smell of dead fish.

We stuck out our thumbs to catch a ride north. Cars and trucks whizzed by. We baked for hours under the heat lamp of the California sun. We were pummeled by pebbles kicked up by passing motorists. Sluggo shouted over the blaring horns and whoosh of traffic, "Nobody sees us! We've got to get their attention!"

Sluggo was an elf-sized shorty and ridiculously athletic. He climbed up my back, stood on my shoulders, and stuck out his thumb. Within minutes, a rusted VW camper van pulled over.

We strapped on our backpacks and ran to the van, occupied by two of the world's smelliest, filthiest hippies. The van reeked of body odor, pot and cigarette smoke, stale beer, and a rancid half-eaten pizza covered with black flies. Forever optimistic, Sluggo and I agreed that the stench was a gift in disguise that would prepare us for the even worse stench awaiting us at the fish cannery three thousand miles north.

The stoned and shirtless driver handed us a joint. "Welcome to The Mystery Ship, man. I'm Nelson." He gestured to his partner in the shotgun seat. "This here's Bogart, our navigator. We're headed to Seattle. You?"

Sluggo and I whooped and high-fived. We couldn't believe our luck. "Seattle?" I yelled. "No shit? We're hitching to Alaska. You guys made our day!" Later, we'd kick ourselves for not adding, "And almost got us killed."

We passed the joint to Bogart. True to his name, Bogart held onto the doobie with his brown-stained fingertips and smoked it down to a charred roach, the hot nub at the end of a joint responsible for thousands of finger burns.

He reached into the glovebox and used a red crayon to draw our route on a fold-out map of the west coast. I detected a Southern drawl, maybe from Louisiana or Mississippi. "Lookie hea boys. We got 'bout a thousand miles of adventures ahead of us between this hea Saucy Lido and Skeedaddle. Y'all pay for gas and we'll getcha there. You copacetic?"

"You bet we're copacetic!" Sluggo blurted without giving the arrangement a second thought. Between us, we had $200 in cash to get to Alaska. He just promised to donate about half of that to fuel The Mystery Ship's sail north on a questionable course with Captain Nelson and First Mate Bogart.

Four hours later, The Mystery Ship cruised up the exit ramp in Garberville, the heart of the great Northern California redwoods. Nelson drove us through Garberville's two-block main street and into a maze of serpentine two-lane roads. Day dissolved into night as we entered the shadowy forest of towering redwood giants.

We began to understand why Nelson named the microbus The Mystery Ship. I started to worry. "Where are we headed? Campground? We've got plenty of freeze-dried beef stroganoff for the four of us." No response. Sluggo piped in, "Or mac 'n cheese. Whichever's cool with you guys."

The continuing silence got to me. There was something slightly unnerving about driving deep into a primeval forest in a dilapidated van with two possible serial killers.

Bogart finally broke the silence. "Almost theya, man. Just makin' a quick stop to pick up a package." *A package?* I thought. We hadn't seen a house for the past ten miles, no less a post office. We had left the asphalt and were headed deeper into the redwoods on a narrow dirt jeep trail. Fallen limbs scraped the sides of the van.

The trail nearly disappeared when a chain-link fence appeared around a curve on the fern-covered forest floor. Nelson hopped out of the driver-side door. Bogart followed, carrying a drawstring canvas sack. They approached the padlocked gate. I noticed movement up in a redwood tree just beyond the fence. A shabby-looking guard with matted dreadlocks, and a shotgun slung over his shoulder, scurried down a ladder from his lookout post.

"Good to see ya, Nels."

"Great to be back, Mad Dog."

"Jake got the package all ready for you. Hold on."

Mad Dog opened a trapdoor hidden under a thick layer of fallen redwood needles on the forest floor. He handed two bulging duffle bags to Nelson. Bogart handed over the sack. "It's awwl in theya, Dawg Man. Nice doin' binness witcha."

When Nelson and Bogart turned to get back in the van, Mad Dog caught sight of Sluggo and me watching the transaction from the back seat. "Just a minute, man. Who's in the van?" He aimed his shotgun at the windshield. "Nobody comes here without Jake's ok. You trying to get us busted?"

Nelson called to us. "Come on out, boys. Meet Mad Dog." While meeting anyone named after a rabid Doberman didn't make my bucket list, we crept out of the camper's sliding door and slowly stepped toward the gate.

Bogart introduced us. "Thissa hea's our two top dee-stributors, Phil Harmonic and Slug Buggy. They's as tight-lipped as stuffed possums fixed to a chimney shelf. Ain't that right, boys?" We nodded in agreement, as quiet as roadkill. "They's a'gonna sell every last seed 'n bud in Skeedaddle so's we can keep a'comin' back for mo' and make Jake happier 'n a tick on a fat hound dawg."

Mad Dog bought Bogart's bogus story, lock, stock, and gun barrel. We climbed back into the van and beelined it for Skeedaddle.

Sluggo and I were only on the road for one day and, by association, had already begun to build a reputation as top drug runners for the Nelson and Bogart West Coast Weed Syndicate.

Like fish, Nelson and Bogart began to smell even worse after three days. We couldn't wait to disembark The Mystery Ship and get to Alaska. But how?

We abandoned our plan to hitchhike fifteen hundred more

miles up the remote Alaska-Canada highway, where a lot of things could *really* go wrong.

The Mystery Ship would be a five-star luxury trip compared to trying to flag down rides in the Canadian wilderness where grizzlies and wolves outnumbered cars and trucks by 1000:1. The idea of fighting off snarling forest animals with sticks, stones, and bags of freeze-dried camp food wasn't appealing compared to, say, flying Alaska Airlines where flight attendants in Eskimo-inspired suits served free bags of roasted peanuts.

The weed brothers dropped us off at the Seattle airport. We wrote personal checks for one-way tickets to Anchorage. Our checking accounts were reduced to all piggy and no bank. After paying the extortion money for Nelson's and Bogart's gas, Sluggo and I had $109.87 in cash to hold us over until we received our first paychecks from the fish cannery.

When we walked off the plane in Anchorage, Bob and Laurie met us at the gate, along with a stuffed ten-foot-tall Kodiak brown bear standing on its hind legs. Some Bureau of Tourism genius chose the taxidermied monster to greet visitors with its flesh-ripping smile. A nice addition would have been a speech bubble coming out of the bear's mouth inscribed with *Welcome to Alaska, where the weak are killed and eaten.*

Bob and Laurie drove us to a forested campground near the center of Anchorage, our temporary home until the cannery jobs came through.

We never considered that a bright orange tent might be a poor choice of colors at 61o N latitude near the top of the world where the midnight sun does shine at midnight as promised. At two o'clock in the morning, Sluggo and I were still wide awake.

The inside of our tent glowed like the hollowed-out core of a candlelit Halloween pumpkin. Worse yet, we discovered a fact widely known to entomologists but not to us.

Mosquitos are drawn to the color orange like flying magnets. A buzzing swarm of bloodsuckers infiltrated our tent.

Alaskan mosquitos are giants compared to their southern cousins. Relatively speaking, if mosquitos in the Midwest are sparrows, Alaskan mosquitos are Pterodactyls.

We zipped up the screen and stuffed socks into any minuscule openings the biting buggers might enter. But they still slipped through our defenses with the devil-may-care enthusiasm of a squadron of hyped-up kamikaze pilots. We hunkered down, buried our heads inside our sleeping bags, and chose the possibility of death by suffocation over death by a thousand proboscis punctures.

Later that morning, we woke to the sound of someone unzipping our tent screen. "Good morning, campers!" Laurie dropped by to see how we fared through the night that wasn't night. "I put a pot of coffee on the fire. Ready when you are."

We joined Laurie—statuesque, shoulder-length dark hair, earthy, dressed in a red-checkered flannel shirt and faded blue jeans—and sat on log rounds around the rock fire pit. She cracked up. "Oh, man, look at you two. I see you've met our state bird. Looks like he pecked up your faces pretty bad."

I looked at myself in the reflection of a shiny tin camping plate. The little devils bypassed the *toes* in mosqui*toes* and congregated on what was formerly my face. A constellation of inflamed welts itched something fierce as if an ant colony had converged for a pub crawl across the dirt mounds of my cheeks.

Laurie continued. "I just heard from the guy who does the hiring at the cannery. He said to hold tight. We've all got jobs, but it may be a couple of weeks before they start canning."

Sluggo and I seized the change of events as a vacation opportunity. We had two weeks to explore Alaska before we would become seafood executioners at the King Salmon slaughterhouse.

Our hitchhiking trip to Alaska's Mount McKinley National Park (now known as Denali) began with a weather-beaten pickup truck and driver that had both led a hard-scrabble arctic life.

Jacob reached across the cab of the old battered Ford truck and pushed open the door with his calloused hand. "Come on in." To make room for us, he picked up a whole salmon from the bench seat and asked, "Hungry?"

We were famished but declined the breakfast of unskinned sushi. Jacob chewed off a chunk of raw salmon, a meal as commonplace as biting the thigh of a dead cow for a steak dinner. He casually placed the fish on the cracked dashboard and scratched his shaggy dark red beard, dripping with fish oil.

"Where are you guys headed?"

"Mount McKinley," Sluggo answered with excited anticipation.

"You're gonna love it up there. That's where I train for the Iditarod with my sled dogs. I can drive you as far as my turnoff, only about 100 miles from the park."

The truck bed was piled high with burlap sacks of crunchy kibble for his pack of 20 Siberian Huskies, Alaskan Malamutes, and Canadian Eskimo dogs. Over the next four hours, Jacob the Musher regaled us with stories about his sled-dogs-of-the-Yukon calamities.

"About 40 miles in, the wind howled like a freight train. The blizzard came on us quick, a whiteout. The lead dogs couldn't see. Neither could I. They cut a corner too fast. The sled tipped over. I struggled to hold on. Otherwise, I'd be left out there to die.

"The dogs dragged me for a quarter mile. When I finally flipped the sled upright, they headed down a steep slope straight toward the river. That's when I knew we were in trouble.

"It was late November. The ice wasn't thick enough to hold me, the sled, and the pack. The farther we rode across the river, the deeper we sank. If it wasn't for a few ice flows, we would have gone all the way through and been swept downriver.

"We finally reached the other side. When we pulled the sled out of the river, I saw a herd of elk waiting there. They ran and we followed behind. Then they disappeared. We kept going and arrived at one of the most beautiful sights I've ever seen—an old abandoned miner's cabin. I built a fire. We dried out. I slept like a pup, warmed by the pack."

Jacob's story shattered the fragile remains of our sense of safety. We stared through the windshield and wondered what we had gotten ourselves into. We were two city kids about to hike in the wild, where either compassionate elk or a million ways to die awaited us.

As promised, Jacob dropped us at his turnoff on Highway 358, a two-lane road through some of Alaska's most rugged terrain between Anchorage and Fairbanks. Snowcapped peaks poked through cottony clouds, thanks to the sun, which forgot to tell the mountains that winter was over.

Miles of open tundra and boulders stretched between us and the mountain range ahead. In the span of an hour, a passing big rig was the only sign of civilization we encountered. If a grizzly sniffed us out, we had no place to hide in the treeless landscape. For all we knew, an atomic blast could have wiped out humanity and left us behind to live off the land, the last two college kids on Earth.

We sat propped up against our backpacks on the side of the road and waited for another truck, any truck, to give us a ride to

McKinley. We both dozed off. I dreamt that we were camped and carried off by a mosquito the size of a 747 jumbo jet. When it released Sluggo over an erupting volcano, the low rumble of an engine and an old codger's voice interrupted my nightmare.

"You boys alright?" he called out the window of his mud-crusted International Harvester Scout.

"Yes, sir," I replied to the kindly grandpa behind the wheel. "We're headed to McKinley. Can you give us a lift?"

"Sure thing. I took you for dead lying on the road like that. Hop in."

Chester's spotless khaki shirt, matching creased trousers, and brimmed cap spoke volumes about the no-frills man behind the outfit. An octogenarian bush pilot, Chester was all substance, no flash. Substance kept him and his passengers alive through blizzards, high-mountain wind shears, and rescues on ice-locked lakes deep in the wilds.

Chester and "panic" were Alaska's polar opposites. He piloted by the book, including chapters he wrote in his memory about avoiding what he called "bush league" mistakes.

Like Jacob, Chester had stories to tell.

"I flew two fishermen to my floatplane camp on the Kenai River. If you want to catch big rainbow trout, fish where the bears fish. They know the best spots and the Kenai's one of 'em.

"We set out in my drift boat. I told 'em to watch out for brown bears and to give their line plenty of slack if a bear went after a fish they hooked. Pretty soon, one of the fellers snagged a huge trout on his fly rod. When I saw that Rainbow break the surface, it looked to be at least 30 inches.

"All the splashin' attracted the attention of a big ol' brown bear and her cubs feedin' in the berry bushes. She charged down the bank and went after the fish. I calmly reminded the feller to let out plenty of line, but he got all caught up in the excitement. He kept reelin' in,

determined not to let that trophy fish get away. Problem was, the bear wasn't about to let that fish go, either. The faster that feller reeled in, the faster the bear swam toward the boat. She was closin' in fast. If she reached us, we'd have found ourselves in a pickle. And pickles ain't my cup of tea.

"That bear came within spittin' distance of the boat when I reached over and cut the line. The trout turned around and goldarn if it didn't swim right into that bear's mouth. The bear turned around, too, and headed back to shore where her two cubs feasted on the dinner of all trout dinners."

Sluggo and I stared ahead into the Alaskan wilderness, agog. Jacob's sled dog saga riveted us. Now Chester had recanted a story akin to Disney actor Fess Parker re-telling a death-defying frontier story from the life of Daniel Boone. Alaska turned back our clock. Living in the past became a lot more exciting than the modern present we'd left behind in California.

Highway 385 could have qualified as one of Alaska's loneliest highways. We hadn't seen another car or truck pass us in more than an hour. Over a fifty-mile stretch, only one sign of human life appeared on the horizon: the Tundra Bar and Grill. Chester chuckled as we whizzed past the chinked-log watering hole.

"What gives, Chester?" I asked. "Seems like that place meant something to you."

"Yes, sir, The Tundra brings back some mighty good memories. Only bar within miles. Hardly anybody stops. Except for that night me and Victor did."

Chester's eyes darted back and forth, recalling each scene that joined the fond-memories section in the library stacks of his mind.

·   ·   ·

"It's like this, boys. I flew with my co-pilot, Victor. We were on our way to pick up a load of snowshoe rabbit pelts from a skinner in Fairbanks. Our course followed Highway 385 north. The weather turned bad. Storm clouds settled in. Victor looked down, spotted The Tundra, and suggested we land. The only landing strip was this highway. So that's where we put down the Cessna. We taxied into the parking lot and went into the bar, which was as empty as a grizzly's innards after a winter nap.

"The bartender told us he didn't know how much longer he could stay in business, what with the low number of passersby stoppin' in. Over the next few hours, practically everyone driving up and down 385 pulled into the lot. They'd never seen a plane parked at a bar and stopped in to find out how it came to be there.

"By dinner time, the bar and restaurant were packed. Folks stood three-deep at the bar. Dinner tables were a two-hour wait.

"The bartender, who was also the owner and cook, hadn't seen that much business since it was designated a post for the firefighters during the 1950's tundra blaze. He told us our drinks were on the house for as long as we kept the plane in the lot.

"Victor and I woke up on the barroom floor the next morning, dragged ourselves out to the plane, and started the engine. We scouted out the highway in both directions. The runway looked clear. Well, as clear as our bloodshot eyes could see. By the time we reached take-off speed, a propane tanker truck came over a rise in the road. Our landing gear barely missed the tank, filled with enough fuel to blow us to kingdom come.

"We made it to Fairbanks, where we picked up the pelts and a rabbit's foot for good luck. It's been with me on every flight since."

Chester reached into his shirt pocket and handed us his rabbit's foot. At 80, he had begun to give things away to people who valued his keepsakes and would pass along his stories.

We needed all the luck we could get when Chester dropped

us at the Visitor's Center in Mount McKinley National Park. Sluggo and I were bound for an unknown destination where creatures bit, gnawed, and chased ill-equipped city folk saddled with ponderous backpacks and underwhelming survival skills. What could possibly go wrong?

We boarded a park shuttle van in search of the hiking trail that a ranger had recommended at the visitor's center. I couldn't help but notice that we were the only hikers not wearing long pants, long-sleeved shirts, and pith helmets draped with mosquito nets large enough to snag a Bald Eagle. Too late. We placed our over-developed sense of confidence in a spray can of mosquito repellant that we bought in Anchorage after camping at the Battle of Bullsquito Run.

The bus driver called out our stop at a remote section of the road. "McKinley River Bar Trail!" No one else got off the bus. I wondered if they knew something we didn't. They did.

Sluggo and I walked across the road to the trailhead sign. The ranger failed to inform us that it was a wild trail, meaning a trail that wasn't actually a trail. No human- or animal-made dirt path. No boot prints of other hikers. No trail arrows to point us in the right direction. Alaska had a cruel sense of humor, and we were the butts of her arctic joke.

We saw Mt. McKinley far off in the distance, soaring above his range of brother peaks that spanned the horizon. With no trail to follow, we headed toward the huge mountain and used it as our guide star. The only thing that separated us from McKinley was everything we didn't want to hike through.

We trudged into a meadow of waist-high scrub bushes. Our legs disappeared under the dense thicket of prickly branches. They clawed at our uncovered legs and tugged at our backpacks as if to warn us, *Turn back, you fools!*

About a mile in, my feet began to sink into grassy mud as thick and slippery as creamed spinach. We had entered a bog disguised under the meadow's blanket of shrubbery. Something cold and slimy slithered across my exposed shin above the boot.

Mutant-sized iridescent dragonflies helicoptered over us in a scouting formation. We crept forward on a moving carpet of croaking toads.

Sluggo struggled through the bushes in front of me. He stopped abruptly, stepped back, cupped his hand to my ear, and whispered, "We have company. Bullwinkle at twelve o'clock. Don't make any noise."

I screamed. "Run!"

A bull moose more massive than a draft horse munched on willow bushes dead ahead of us. The powerful herbivore swung its enormous head in our direction and lowered his antlers. They resembled gargantuan outstretched hands capable of tossing us into the air like ragdolls.

Unlike our labored, step-by-step hike into the bush, we ran with the swiftness of Olympic hurdlers, jumping over bushes and out of the meadow in leaps and bounds. The moose stayed behind and ignored us, more interested in eating his salad of willow leaves than chasing a couple of lily-livered hikers.

I have no idea how long or far we ran. When we felt safe enough to stop and catch our breath, we found ourselves off-course on the stony bank of a river with no park road or Mt. McKinley in sight.

Sluggo shot his fists in the air and pranced a happy elfin dance. "What a rush! Man, was that intense!"

I panted, "A rush? Are you crazy? We could have been trampled! Now we're lost. How do we get back to the road?"

"The road? We can find it later when we get to higher ground across the river. We came to see Alaska. This is Alaska on steroids, the spot people travel millions of miles to see from places like Outer Mongolia! We can't go back now. We'll make our own trail! We'll camp under a billion stars. We'll set traps and make squirrel hats!"

Sluggo could be pretty persuasive. He always tossed an absurd third item into his sales pitches to throw me off and win me over. His enthusiasm was so contagious, that he could sell socks to a snake. Plus, he was an Eagle Scout who knew how to blaze a trail and came prepared with a map and compass. Who was I to disagree?

He led us along the glacial riverbank. At a wide bend in the channel, I glanced at Sluggo and thought he'd literally lost his head. A black cloud of swarming mosquitos had almost completely veiled his face. He couldn't see my head either. We were both trapped in the eyes of swirling mosquito cyclones.

I looked down and saw the ravenous biters scatter like puffs of sawdust under every footfall of my boots. Sluggo scrambled down the bank, hugged his backpack as a flotation device, and dove head-first into the icy-cold river. The fast-moving current swept him downstream. I dove in after him.

He eventually paddled to the side, grabbed the limb of a fallen tree, and held on tight. I reached out and latched onto his leg.

We pulled ourselves to shore and slogged up the bank into a stand of aspen trees. Both of us fell to the ground and laughed our asses off. Near-death experiences can do that to a person.

A stiff, warm breeze blasted away the godless mosquito marauders. Both of us stripped off our wet clothes and hung them on tree branches to air dry. We could finally relax without being eaten alive. Sluggo and I sat on a soft bed of aspen leaves on the forest floor.

We breathed in the moment, two friends who courageously explored the vast Alaskan wilderness. Naked.

All along our route, Big Game left their calling card paw prints and scat piles. I interpreted this as the animal kingdom's way of sending the message, *You're in our territory. Watch your back.* Other than the moose we almost startled on the first day, man-killing creatures hid and probably laughed at us from behind nearby trees and bushes. I concluded that the answer to the age-old question, *Do bears shit in the woods?* was *Yes, as long as nobody's watching.*

Two weeks later, we celebrated our last night in the wilderness camped at a peaceful mountain lake, a half-day hike from the park road and van that would carry us back to civilization. By then, any fears about wild animals attacking us had evaporated. By God, we believed we'd graduated to wilderness experts. We could damn well sleep outside under the stars without a care or worry.

That was a mistake.

Sluggo and I had fallen into our nightly bedtime routine. We sprayed ourselves with mosquito repellant, slipped into our mummy bags beside the fire, gazed up at the billions of stars he'd promised, and slipped on our sunglasses when we were falling asleep to block out the twilight of the midnight sun.

I woke up at daybreak to something sniffing my hair and ears. I opened my eyes but couldn't see. The unseen beast's hot breath had steamed up the lenses of my sunglasses. Like a terrified five-year-old hiding under the covers from Ape Woman, I played dead, hoping whatever it was would leave us alone and spare our lives. The retreating clomp, clomp, clomp of hoof beats rumbled through the hard, rocky ground.

When my sunglasses defogged, I crooked my neck to get a view of the mystery guest in our camp. We'd come full circle. The bull moose we had surprised at the beginning of the hike had tracked us. He smelled the last of the trail mix inside our backpacks hung high in a tree.

I whispered to Sluggo, who was half asleep on the opposite side of the fire pit. "Pssst. Pssst. Slug. Wake up." He turned toward me and yawned. I waved my hand to hush him up and kept whispering. "Shhhhhh. We have company. Look. Bullwinkle's back."

We watched as the monstrous moose lowered his head and antlers and shook the tree. He pushed the tree trunk back and forth for a half hour. Eagle Scout Sluggo's rope knots held. The backpacks swung back and forth but never broke free.

Bullwinkle finally gave up, looked back at us, and disappeared into the forest with a parting snort, as if to say, *Farewell. It's been real. Now get off my land.*

When we arrived back in Anchorage, Laurie informed us that the canning season was delayed and still weeks away. With no jobs and almost no money, we cut our Alaska summer short. Our parents wired airfare to our checking accounts, which we promised to pay back when we landed more predictable and less fragrant summer jobs below the 49th parallel.

Bob and Laurie dropped us off at the Anchorage airport. We checked our backpacks at the ticket counter, his to San Francisco and mine to Colorado.

We strolled out to the gate and talked about the highlights of our adventure: Drug running with Nelson and Bogart on The Mystery Ship; sleepless nights in our orange tent; murderous mosquitoes; meeting Alaska's frontier characters; surviving two weeks in the wilderness; and mystical encounters with Bullwinkle the moose.

All in all, it was the best and worst of adventures. Before we parted ways, Sluggo and I had one piece of unfinished business.

We paused at the terminal's stuffed Kodiak bear, snorted farewell to him, and boarded our planes for destinations where the weak were not killed and eaten.

24

SINK RATS

"A cult following is a nice way of saying very few people like you."
- Martin Mull

Robert Redford worked there as a janitor in college. Dan Aykroyd and Madeleine Albright ate there. A college girl spilled her raspberry smoothie on Barack Obama's perfectly pressed Valentino dress slacks there. Guy Fieri filmed an episode of *Diners, Drive-Ins and Dives* there. "There" is and was The Sink, Boulder's classic college dive bar and restaurant, established more than a century ago in 1923. What I saw there in 1973 and 1974 as a beer-tender was nothing short of the Rocky Mountain capital of hippiedom.

More than a burger joint, The Sink could have easily been a quirky art museum. Low ceilings are still covered in a scrawl of indecipherable overlapping signatures of graduates and celebrities, signed with black and red Sharpie pens. Murals cover every wall, painted with caricatures of imaginary creatures, academic characters, and famous figures like Albert Einstein and Alfred E. Neuman.

Colorful cartoons capture the freethinking college whimsy,

activism, and philosophy of the 1960s and '70s. One portrays a male painter in a CU art class. He asked a female subject, "Do you mind if I paint you in the nude?" She shot back, "Put your clothes back on right now."

Back in the '70s, diehard patrons were called Sink Rats. They were nocturnal creatures most active after the sun went down. Sink Rats often entered the door in packs, scurried to bar stools, and foraged for free food scraps.

On Friday and Saturday nights, my job was to pour pitchers of beer continuously for six hours. So many college kids packed the house that anyone who passed out never fell to the floor. The crowd propped them up like plastered mannequins leaning together in a department store display window.

I filled pitchers of Coors, Budweiser, Pabst Blue Ribbon, Olympia, and Falstaff from five taps and served them through the beer window, a square, shoulder-width hole in the wall. The low window was at chest-level height, giving the impression that the people ordering beer were headless. Likewise, they could only see my chest. That forced both of us to bend down so we could fill orders face-to-face.

Their chests provided no clue what their faces might look like until they leaned down and faced me through the window. I can't tell you how many mismatched chests and faces surprised me on any given night. A college guy in a baggy blue jean shirt turned out to be a spectacularly gorgeous co-ed and dead ringer for actress Raquel Welch. A busty girl was actually an overweight guy and Culinary Arts student packing size 42 man boobs.

One chest topped them all. It wore an orange and black striped rugby shirt. The shirt filled the window like a tightly pulled curtain. I leaned down and spoke to the shirt. "Can I help you?"

I came face-to-face with a square-jawed giant. His head was connected to a neck almost as thick as my thigh. I couldn't tell where his neck ended and his head began. They blended like a super-human neck surveying me with menacing eyeballs.

The Giant squinted. His threatening glare informed me that my remaining time on earth might be limited. "Your name Caragol?" "Y-y-y-yes," I stammered.

He reached through the window with a hand comparable to an oversized oven mitt, gripped my shirt collar with his fist, and pulled me through the window.

The whole bar watched as he lifted me off the ground with his bulging arm and pinned my bent neck against the ceiling. A series of past transgressions flashed through my mind, much like the experience of hospital patients moments before their last breath.

Was the Giant the former boyfriend of a girl I dated and unintentionally mistreated? Or worse yet, could he be her angry brother who found out that I was the one who unknow-ingly robbed her of her virginity?

The crowd roared. The joke was on me. The Giant had a name. Greg lowered me to the floor. He and another Sigma Delta brother from the Nebraska chapter were visiting Boulder and had stopped by the house. Greg played defensive lineman for the Corn Huskers. Years of working in the fields, combined with the DNA of a giant, formed a human being of unusual size, strength, and humor.

My fraternity brothers asked him to do the deed that temporarily changed my life and underwear. They all stood around me, doubled over, laughing to tears.

It's been said that true friends are not easily found. And that the measure of a true friend is a friend who's comfortable enough to mess with you. That was exactly what I discovered that night at The Sink. They were true friends who made me feel like a giant at the hands of a giant. For the first time in my life, they made me feel like a normal person, imperfections and all.

Life in the '60s and '70s was not all free love, peace, pussy willows and cattails. We were a generation of seekers. We sought belonging, self-awareness, identity, and whatever else gurus offered to elevate our consciousness to a higher plane.

We tried Buddhism, Daoism, the Jesus Movement, Hinduism, Sikhism, and Humanism. We revered spiritual leaders, including but not limited to the Dalai Lama, Ram Das, and Cheech and Chong.

Some fell prey to cult leaders. More than 900 followers of The People's Temple perished in Guyana after drinking cyanide Kool-Aid under the order of fanatical leader Jim Jones. Reverend Sun Myong Moon lured young seekers to his Unification Church compounds. Mass marriage ceremonies of couples who had never met each other were matched by Moon and destined to a life of servitude. They were prevented from any outside contact with family and friends (like Hell Week at the fraternity without a term limit).

In the 1970s, one of these radical counterculture groups took up shop in Boulder, the STP Family. STP was an extremely powerful hallucinogen. Unlike a spiritual group, STP members were aggressive and violent addicts, drunks, panhandlers, dealers, and ripoff artists. They popped STP tablets and any other drugs they could score. Their glassy eyes transmitted a crazy Charlie Manson madness. They were primitives, the Neanderthal drug tribe of the counterculture.

You could spot them by their clothes, rancid denim shirts and pants patched with leather, scraps of cloth, and an STP emblem, the logo of the STP fuel treatment company. They often decorated their clothing with the skulls of small animals. Nothing said "accessorize" like a chipmunk skull pendant.

They were dirty, foul-smelling, and violent, unlike other counterculture kids in Boulder. They drank heavily, mostly cheap wine and a concoction of grape Kool-Aid mixed with Everclear grain alcohol called Purple Jesus.

In Colorado, they lived in the mountains in tents, lean-tos, and abandoned cabins. The STP family claimed to be mountain men and women and bragged about killing bears. They probably made that up. But they did wear bear-claw-and-tooth necklaces, probably shoplifted at a Navajo swap meet.

More bizarrely, eyewitnesses claimed that The Family ate their dead during gruesome ceremonies. Granted, these witnesses had imbibed large quantities of Purple Jesus, so they might have imagined that the chicken legs served at the funeral after-party were the legs of small family members.

One Friday afternoon, a wild-eyed STP stoner barged through the Sink's batwing saloon doors. He stormed up to co-worker Ken and frantically asked, "Have you seen my purple turtle? The one with the pink polka dots?" Ken thanked him for the detailed description so he wouldn't mistake the stoner's purple turtle for the slow-moving crowd of other yellow, pink, and turquoise striped turtles chugging pints of Coors at the bar. "Sure," Ken said. "He crawled in here about an hour ago. He's in the back room."

As Ken wiped down a table in the front room, Turtle Man returned, cradling something under his torn flannel shirt. He shouted to Ken on his way out the door, "Thanks, man! You did me a solid. Jasper's messed up, but I think he's gonna make it." Turns out Jasper was his left shoe.

The real trouble started when the STP family worked together as a pack. During the lunch shift one Colorado blue-sky summer day, six of them marched into the restaurant, spread out, and accosted booths of laid-back college kids.

The Family helped themselves to whatever our customers were eating and drinking. They snatched burgers off plates and gnawed off bites. They chugged customers' beers. In five minutes, they consumed half of our patrons' lunches and beverages and marched back out the front door, believing themselves to be invincible, immortal, and beyond consequences.

Overconfidence had backfired a few other times in history. We would soon re-enact a Sink version of the Gunfight at the O.K. Corral.

Our 24-year-old manager, Robbie, called our crew together of eight cooks, bartenders, and busboys. Robbie wore a floppy Jimi Hendrix hat and had moved to Boulder from San Antonio, Texas. He grew up near The Alamo and knew a thing or two about arming for a battle. The STP family would return. Robbie developed a plan to defeat them.

Robbie: "Let's hit 'em at the front door with everything we've got. Ideas?"

D.B.: "How about a mop bucket of boiling water?"

Robbie: "I like it. Next."

Ken: "Is the fire extinguisher charged? I'd love to freeze their faces off."

Robbie. "Yes, and done."

Me: "I got dibs on the ammonia bottles. Spray 'em in eyes, I will."

Robbie: "Go! The rest of you find whatever you can to get rid of these assholes."

Robbie assumed the lookout position. Around 4 p.m., he sounded the alarm. "Get ready. Here they come. Take your positions."

We formed a semicircle one room away from the entrance and prepared to strike. The leader of The Family pushed open the batwing doors, followed by his minions of smelly believers.

When they were all inside, we opened fire with a simultaneous barrage of boiling water and cleaning products. They ran out the door, boiled and drenched, eyes on fire with ammonia and fire extinguisher foam.

The next morning, all of the windows in The Sink were

smashed out with rocks. Most of the windows have remained bricked or ice-blocked for the past 50 years.

Our Gunfight at The Sink Corral taught me something that's stuck with me for 50 years.

Most people are excellent human beings. A few others will always be mean and nasty. Talk to them. Or ignore them. But always keep an ammonia bottle handy, just in case.

❦ 25 ❦
ANIMAL IN THE HOUSE

"Seven years of college down the drain.
Might as well have joined the fucking Peace Corps."
- Bluto Blutarsky, *Animal House*

I
f John Belushi and Evel Knievel fathered May West's surrogate baby, the little terror would grow up to be fraternity brother and 1970s University of Colorado legend, Wild Bill. The stories are endless. Never satisfied by merely crossing the line, Wild Bill pole vaulted over it—occasionally naked and lathered in shaving cream.

His charismatic, steel-bodied, combat-boot-wearing presence was felt by everyone when he entered a room. Like Genghis Khan at a lady's knitting bee, Wild Bill found the ideal haven to invade. Boulder's peace-loving hippies and goody-two-shoes John Denver lookalikes never saw Bill coming. Until they did. And then they either laughed or ran in the opposite direction.

On one such occasion, Wild Bill sat next to an attractive co-ed at a bar in Nederland, an anti-establishment nomad community up the mountain from Boulder. Her paisley mini dress, beaded vest, square blue granny sunglasses, and peace symbol headband screamed "hippie girl."

Wild Bill removed one of his black combat boots and plunked it on the bar.

"If you can guess my boot size, I'll buy you a beer."

"Far out," she replied, eager to play along. "I'll say you're a... a size...um...11?"

Wild Bill hollered, "Barkeep. Bring me and this fox two bottles of your finest plasma." He used "plasma" to describe alcohol in any form, an elixir to him as vital to human life as blood itself. She turned to the bartender and playfully clarified the order, "What a trippy guy, huh? Make it two beers, brother."

Pleased with herself for correctly guessing Bill's boot size, she raised her frosty green bottle of Heineken in a toast. "Here's to the Freaks. Peace, man." They clinked bottles. She poured hers into a beer glass. Wild Bill poured his into the combat boot. He tilted his head back and let the beer cascade like a waterfall into the pool that was his mouth.

She shifted nervously on the barstool. "Wow, man, *that's* a first."

"Nah," he objected. "I've chugged plasma from boots, shoes, slippers, and strained through a sock. But I'm guessing you haven't seen *this*."

He tapped the rim of his unused beer glass on the bar, broke off a piece, ground it between his molars, and swallowed. She slid off the barstool and tiptoed out the door. He ordered another plasma and continued eating the beer glass.

I stopped asking myself, *Why did Wild Bill do this stuff?* when he showed me a 1971 *Sports Illustrated* article about his hero and role model.

Off-the-wall NFL football player Tim Rossovich became famous for his wild pranks. Rossovich jumped naked into birthday cakes, set himself on fire at parties, and posed as modern art in hotel lobbies standing on his head in a bucket of water. Another time, he opened his mouth to make a speech at a team owners' meeting and a sparrow flew out.

I started appreciating Wild Bill as a Rossovich emulator and a never-ending source of original entertainment. Bill was not unlike having Dick Butkus or The Hulk as a friend who never balked when I tagged along to witness his feats of shock and awe.

He raced his motorcycle up the steps of the fraternity house during a rush party and gave recruits free rides around the living room while extolling the benefits of joining Sigma Delta. "You're gonna love this place! The circus comes to town every night!"

I witnessed the aftermath of a head-shaving party with his tribe of fellow conspirators, the Flying Burrito Brothers. They shaved each other's heads while drinking vast quantities of cheap scotch. The more heads they shaved, the more the razor dulled.

The next morning, Wild Bill staggered into the fraternity house, looking like his head got stuck in a meat grinder. The razor cuts were so profuse that his head could have passed for a meatball sub, lacking only the bun.

In some ways, Bill and I were kindred spirits. Boredom was our arch nemesis. When a conversation dragged or a party fizzled, something clicked—or snapped—in his timebomb mind. That telltale *time to liven things up* look in his faraway stare flashed a warning sign.

In the middle of a boring poker game, he was neither winning nor losing, it was not uncommon for Bill to push back from the table, strip off all his clothes, and run naked out the door to some unknown destination.

He sprinted like a cheetah. Without clothes and wind resistance, he was almost impossible to catch until he ran up to a front porch and rang the doorbell. I would not be surprised if Bill heard a freakshow barker inside his head announce,

"Ladies and gentlemen, step right up. See the amazing Wild Bill hang an enormous moon in all of his glory!"

The porch light became Bill's spotlight; the door, his stage curtain. One thing about Bill: He could be as charming as he was crude. When the flabbergasted college renter opened the door and overcame the initial shock, he or she generally enjoyed the show. Bill's absurd dialogue often produced a smile.

"Good evening. My name is Bill. I just dropped by to let you know there's a beautiful full moon tonight." Then he turned about-face to drive home the point.

His naked outings regularly included props. Holding a hot dog, he asked a startled house renter, "Pardon me. Do you have any Grey Poupon?"

Wearing only a Richard Nixon mask and combat boots, he inquired, "Excuse me. Have you seen Tricky Dick?"

Wild Bill was also hard to miss at Colorado football games. No one but Bill knew why it seemed like a good idea to dress in a gorilla costume and sneak a pony keg of beer into the stadium in a baby carriage. Was the costume a brilliant distraction from the shiny steel barrel of beer hidden under the baby blanket? Did he imagine that no one dared stop someone who was out of touch enough to wear a gorilla outfit to a game where the team mascot was a buffalo?

Knowing Wild Bill, he probably dressed like a gorilla pushing a keg stroller simply because the idea popped into his head. So, he believed it was meant to be on a cosmic level others would never understand.

Shortly after shaving his head, Wild Bill approached me and my fraternity brother, Tad, with a scheme to steal a few "mementos" from a police car. We reluctantly agreed to drive him to the car's location but refused to steal the mementos, partially because we had no idea what constituted a law enforcement memento or why we would want one.

Bill dressed for the mission in his signature camo T-shirt, drab olive army fatigues, and combat boots. The three of us piled into my car, a black 1951 Nash Ambassador sporting the curved shape of a deep-sea Orca, and zipped across town to Baseline Road, a main thoroughfare through town.

The Texaco station on Baseline serviced all of the police cars in Boulder's fleet. When we arrived in the dirt lot behind the gas station under cover of darkness, six black-and-whites were parked at the quiet side of the building, all awaiting maintenance.

Wild Bill sprang out of the passenger seat and crawled on his belly toward the police cars with a screwdriver clenched between his teeth as if preparing for a pirate fight. Tad and I stayed back and hid behind a mound of dirt to keep an eye on Bill and whatever mementos he planned on pilfering. He crept out of sight behind one of the cars, like a bald mountain lion hunting its prey.

Tad and I waited while Bill went to work. We suddenly noticed that he wasn't alone. A tall, thin, middle-aged manager wearing a short-sleeved shirt emblazoned with the red Texaco star appeared on the scene. He yelled at Bill and waved his arms in pleading gestures.

Tad jumped into action. "Aw shit. Let's go."

We hopped over the dirt mound and raced to the police cars. The Texaco man warned Bill, "I'm going to ask you again: get out from under that car, or I'll call the police!" Bill ignored him. He was busy unscrewing a police license plate memento.

The manager extended his final offer. "Listen, I know you're a vet. Just get up and I'll let you go."

The shaved head. The camo shirt. The army fatigues. It all added up. Bill's appearance led the manager to conclude that the bald warrior stealing the license plate had just returned from Vietnam and presumably suffered from PTSD.

In the split second the manager's words left his mouth, Wild Bill leaped to his feet and pointed the screwdriver like a switch-blade, ready to slash the terrified manager to ribbons.

Bill barked a threat none of us could have foreseen. "Don't you EVER call me a vet!" If he had calmed down, Bill might have explained his deep respect for veterans and that he didn't feel worthy of the title. No matter. The terrified manager ran into the station, locked the door, and killed the lights. No doubt, he called the police to report a robbery in progress involving an unhinged army veteran wielding a life-threatening Phillips Head screwdriver.

Tad and I dragged Wild Bill toward our getaway car. But not before he shouted, "Wait!" and snatched a cherry-red police bubble off the roof of one of the cars.

When we returned to the fraternity house, Wild Bill marched to the living room, unlocked the glass trophy case reserved for prized fraternity sports trophies, and reverently placed the police car bubble inside.

Bill's memento remained in the case for several days until another idea popped into his head. Anytime friends needed refreshment, Wild Bill opened his mini-fridge and poured them a beer from his conversation piece, the one-of-a-kind police bubble plasma pitcher.

Of all of Wild Bill's public appearances in his birthday suit, one stood out. This time, he did not evade arrest.

In March 1972, a CU sorority held its annual formal party with dates at Boulder's Timber Tavern, a popular bar and restaurant that resembled a log Rocky Mountain hunting lodge.

Sorority sisters and their guests packed the tavern, including their elderly house mother, Mom Reynolds.

At approximately 10:30 PM, Wild Bill and four friends entered the tavern in their birthday suits. Bill, Crazy Harry, Bevins, Biscuit, and Dodi approached the bar, ordered cocktails, and mingled.

Girls in crushed velvet dresses and dates in suits and ties soon discovered that the party had been crashed by a group of college streakers who didn't even attempt to cover their protuberances.

Wild Bill and his friends joined casual conversations with the crowd as if they were attending an afternoon tea party. It would have worked except that they were as naked as jaybirds. And by midnight, they would become jailbirds known as the notorious Timber Tavern Five.

Wild Bill knew Mom Reynolds well. She had previously served as the live-in house mom at the Sigma Delta house and was beloved by all. After living in a fraternity for several years, there was little that offended her. She and Bill reminisced about old times and caught up on events in their lives after she moved into the sorority house.

"Bill, it's good to see you're still up to your old tricks. You always did make life so, let's say, *colorful*. A word to the wise, though. You might put clothes on before someone calls the authorities. I've seen plenty of you boys running around in the nude over the years. It doesn't bother me, but some of the girls might be embarrassed and sound the alarm."

Bill thanked Mom Reynolds for the advice and returned to the bar. The long-haired bartender tipped him off. "You better split, man. The fuzz are on their way." Bill alerted the Timber Tavern Five. They scrambled out to Bill's lime-green Chevy Vega wagon. Sirens a block away pierced the midnight hour.

Of the five, only Crazy Harry was medium-sized. Wild Bill and the other three could easily pass as beefy college football players. They squeezed into the Vega and screeched out of the parking lot.

Cops in the lead car chased in pursuit with red lights flashing and sirens blaring. Wild Bill realized escape was futile and pulled over to the curb. Two more police cars arrived on the scene, one missing a roof bubble.

With guns drawn, the cops ordered The Five to get out of the car and raise their hands in the air. This took some time. The police watched in astonishment as the huge students pushed and pulled their sizable naked bodies out of the cramped Vega.

No strip search was required.

Police handcuffed The Five, loaded them into squad cars, and drove to the Boulder Jail holding station. Upon arrival, officers fingerprinted the criminals and snapped mug shots. Wild Bill smiled for the camera.

The police made the mistake of placing them in adjacent chain-link cell cages. Shortly after officers locked the cage doors, the Timber Tavern Five broke into a soulful rendition of Elvis's "Jailhouse Rock." The hits kept on coming—"Ba-Ba-Ba-Ba-Barbara Ann," "Duke of Earl," "At the Hop," "My Little Teddy Bear," "Rock Around the Clock."

Other inmates joined in, clapping hands, stomping feet, and singing along. They re-enacted the Attica prison riot, only without police hostages and enhanced by a lively *a cappella* doo-wop chorus.

Annoyed guards covered their ears. The cacophony pushed them to the brink. They had enough of the deafening off-key prisoners and released them with orders to report to the courthouse the next day for their arraignment.

Due to the sensitive nature of the case, the judge had the bailiff schedule The Five at the end of the day when no guests or reporters would be in the courtroom.

The judge bore an uncanny likeness to comedian Bob

Newhart, older and grayer but endowed with the same sad Bassett Hound face. He called the court to order and asked The Five to rise and hear the charges.

"Well, boys, it looks like you had quite a night. You're charged with Disturbing the Peace, Disorderly Conduct, Prostitution, and Lewd Acts. How do you plead?"

Wild Bill spoke for the group. "Your judgeship, we plead 'not guilty.' If it pleases the court, may we discuss the case in your chambers?" The judge paused. Knowing that none of the defendants had criminal records, he approved the request. "Very well, young man." He banged the gavel on the sound block. "Court is in recess. Bailiff, escort the defendants to my chambers."

The Five lined up in front of the judge seated behind his imposing antique western desk. He interrogated Bill.

"Son, was it your premeditated intention to disturb the peace at that party?"

"No, sir. If anything, we intended to liven up the party."

"And would you describe your conduct as disorderly?"

"No, sir. We never busted up the place, and I'd say we were polite to everyone we met."

"Did you engage in lewd acts and prostitution?"

"No again, your honor. We did not perform any lewd acts and didn't have sex with anyone at the party. We were 'in and out,' so to speak."

"Be that as it may, my concern is that you have set a precedent. No one wants to see Boulder become a haven for nudists exposing themselves in public. If I let you off scot-free, what will stop other university students from running naked willy-nilly?"

The Five burst out laughing.

"Gentlemen, that was not a double entendre! You are testing my patience!"

Wild Bill intervened. "We apologize, judge. We only

laughed because you have nothing to worry about. No other students will do what we did. Getting naked in public isn't even on their radar. You have our word that we'll never do it again."

The judge tapped his fingertips on the desk pad, watching The Five's eyes for signs of deception.

"All right, then. I'll suspend my ruling. But if your stunt encourages anyone to commit the same offense over the next six months, I'll see you here again—and next time, the court will show no mercy. You're free to go."

To commemorate the victory, The Five placed an anonymous classified ad in the *Boulder Daily Camera*. Large capital letters spelled out a fabricated call to action from Richard Nixon's corrupt vice president, Spiro Agnew, who resigned in disgrace: SPIRO SAYS—FREE THE TIMBER TAVERN FIVE.

The Five graduated and moved out of town. Six months later, more than one thousand students streaked naked across the University of Colorado campus.

None were arrested.

✴ 26 ✺

I DATED MY LITTLE SISTER

"You make me want to be a better man."
- Elliot Garfield, *Goodbye Girl*

"Lent" is the 40-day period of religious fasting before the Easter resurrection of Christ. During Lent, it's not unusual to hear Christians ask each other, "What are you giving up for Lent?" They don't ask out of curiosity. They want to know how their sacrifice stacks up against other giver-uppers.

I mean, why give up something big like a trip to the Bahamas when you can give up something small like not eating chocolate chip cookies on Tuesdays? Of course, there's a reward for making such a sacrifice. By giving up cookies on Tuesdays, you can eat as many cookies as you want the other six days of the week without feeling an iota of guilt.

I wonder: Is giving up any amount of chocolate chip cookies a sacrifice equal to, say, being whipped, crowned with thorns, and nailed to a cross by red-caped Roman centurions? Probably not. That's why overachievers like my college girlfriend gave up big stuff during Lent. Big crazy stuff.

Susie gave up *men*. And truthfully, I couldn't have been happier. Forty days of male deprivation in the prime of her womanhood made me look a bit more attractive as a possible, maybe boyfriend.

I initially questioned the decision of this gorgeous college coed who ditched dating. Was she a serial introvert? Lipstick Lesbian? Escapee from the Sigmund Freud Home for Man-Hating Women?

In fact, Susie turned down dates because she mourned the recent loss of her young father. She went out on a few dates after his death at age 44. But she didn't have fun, assumed her dates didn't either, and took a break from boys.

Susie's father and I were both members of the same fraternity at the University of Colorado, he in the WWII years, me in the hippie years. Hank's fraternal membership automatically qualified Susie to be an honorary Little Sister of our chapter. Exclusive benefits included, among other things, beating beer-guzzling brothers at the Bridge table.

She joined the Gamma Pi sorority and single-handedly raised the grade point average of the house of 80 girls. After her dating hiatus, her sorority sisters returned the favor. They organized a spring fling. Susie would have to find a date to bring to the party. And the girls were prepared to sabotage any excuse that Susie invented to miss the party.

She tried to sign up to work that night at the Harvest House restaurant, where she waitressed part-time. A sorority sister who also worked there took the last unclaimed shift. Not to be outsmarted, Susie invited her older brother, Charlie, to be her date. But another sorority sister had already beaten her to the punch.

With only one day to go before the party, the Gamma Pi's launched an emergency manhunt. What red-blooded college boy could possibly resist Susie's wholesome girl-next-door looks, waist-length waves of blonde *Alice in Wonderland* hair, olive-shaped blue-gray eyes, brilliant mind, and quick wit?

A friend, Debbie D., knew that Susie was a Sigma Delta Little Sister. She called the pay phone in the lobby of the fraternity house. Afro-haired and mustachioed Dave Muncho answered the phone.

"Hello. Sigma Delta. How's it goin'?"

"Is that you, Dave? It's Debbie D. I have an emergency."

"Far out. Wait. That sounds intense. What kind of emergency? I'm not a doctor, just pre-med."

"I need to find a date—fast."

"Are you asking me out, Debs? Weird. I was gonna ask *you* out and..."

"It's not for me."

"You mean *I'm* not for you?"

"No, I mean I need a date for someone else—Susie Blickhahn."

"You want me to date Susie Blickhahn?"

"Dave, STOP! Listen to me. We're throwing a big spring party at our house tomorrow night. Can you ask the guys if anybody wants to go with Susie?"

"Why didn't you just say that? OK. Hold on."

I was playing volleyball outside with a dozen guys. Muncho opened the door and yelled, "Anybody want to go to a party at the Gamma Pi house with Susie Blickhahn tomorrow night?"

Thanks to ADHD, my hand had a mind of its own and spontaneously shot up in the air. "I'll go!" Like little Elton John who said "yes" to piano lessons and the Sundance Kid who said "yes" to robbing banks, the trajectory of my life changed in a split second of "yes."

What was I thinking? My first two years of college were filled with mostly shallow relationships. Susie Blickhahn made me nervous, a girl too deep, too beautiful, too nice, too smart for a knucklehead like me. Plus, her German last name translated to Chicken Watcher. I was chicken, and she'd be watching for me to slip up.

When I entered the Greek-columned sorority house, girls and their dates swarmed the lobby like a buzzing beehive of queens and drones. I spotted Susie waiting in line for the dining room to open. She wore a paisley blouse, sweater vest, and blue jean mini skirt. She waved her arms in an animated conversation with a freckle-faced sorority sister. I took a deep breath, walked up to her, and anxiously stepped off the first-date cliff.

"Hey, Susie, how ya doing?"

"Hi, Phil! Meet my roommate, Annie! We just finished a bottle of Cold Duck!"

Thank God for cheap bubbly made by some marketing guy named André. Both girls flapped their arms in a duck pose, squawked "Quack! Quack!" and laughed so hard their eyes sparkled with André's Cold Duck tears. I was smitten. My goody-two-shoes Little Sister also knew how to have a good time. She had me at "Quack!"

After dinner, Susie and I sang nonsensical opera to the crowd from the top of the steps in the sorority's sunken living room. Couples cuddled up on couches, high-back chairs, and each other. They applauded and howled at the end of our original arias based on operas such as:

Carmen (not *The Toreador Song*): *Toreador, don't spit on the floor, use the cuspidor, that's what it's for!*

La Traviata (not *The Drinking Song*): *Chi-an-ti! Blue Nun-a-cini! Gal-lo pro-fun-do! Rav-i-oli! Spagh-a-tini! Sahhhhhhh-lu-tayyyyy!*

More than a first date, our night together was a fresh start for both of us. I, the shallow serial dater, morphed into a one-girl boyfriend. She, the grieving daughter, hopped out of her boyless tomb.

Neither of us wanted the night to end. After everyone left the party, Susie walked me outside to say goodnight. We held hands, face to face under the porch light, two college kids who magically became one in five short hours. I felt the electricity tingle between us and wasn't about to flip the breaker switch.

She raised her hands to my shoulders. I wrapped my arms around her waist. We kissed a kiss that opened the sky and shook the earth.

"Excuse me," Susie asked the bartender. "Did anyone come in here wearing a scuba outfit?"

"You mean the guy in the wet suit? That guy cracked us up. He danced on the bar like a penguin. Don't know how he pulled it off with those flippers on his feet. He left about five minutes ago. Said he needed to refill his tank."

On my 21st birthday, two weeks after our first date, Susie and her friend Suzie searched for me in bars around Boulder, carrying a chocolate birthday cake she baked for me. I moved fast for a scuba diver out of water in land-locked Colorado.

My roommate, Ken, attended diving classes at the university rec center's indoor pool. I wanted to make a splash on the birthday that marked my official entry ticket to adulthood. He helped me wiggle into the wetsuit and completed the frogman outfit with a mask, snorkel, air tank, fins, and weight belt. Our one-night mission: 21 drinks at 21 dive bars.

Ken drove us in his bright red Chevy Nova to Burger King to fill our stomachs before the birthday marathon. When we walked in, tables of students cheered. Evidently, this was the first time they'd seen a scuba diver in a Burger King.

The 50-ish manager behind the counter looked exhausted,

probably as a result of endless shifts of serving rowdy college kids. A lit cigarette dangled from his lips. The bags under his eyes could have passed as carry-on luggage.

"You made my day. Food's on the house. What'll it be?"

I glanced at the menu board. "Two fish fillet sandwiches, please."

A "Take One" countertop display next to the cash register caught my eye. It held free packets of Zinnia seeds. The promotional connection to Burger King eluded me, but free was free. I ripped the top off a packet, poured the seeds into my mouth, and blew them out through the snorkel.

Unfortunately, a young family behind me had just entered the restaurant. The preppy-looking mother and father hugged their two little girls as a barrage of zinnia seeds rained down on their shell-shocked faces. One of the girls cried, "Mommy, that bad man spit gooey stuff all over my new dress!" We grabbed the sandwiches and ran out the door to our getaway car.

According to eyewitness accounts, the rest of the night involved a variety of antics, and not only at dive bars. I swam the scuba man breaststroke between partners' legs on a crowded dance floor. I surprised couples at a seafood restaurant by popping up from under tables and asking, "So, how's the seabass?" I sang Grand Funk Railroad's "I'm Your Captain" to a group of sailors on shore leave at The Bus Stop, Boulder's only gentlemen's club—and about the only place Susie didn't search for me.

She finally caught up with me at midnight, laying on the carpet in my apartment, dressed in full scuba gear with the yellow air tank on my back and my arms around the vacuum cleaner. I must have thought the vacuum was Susie, only with a longer neck.

I wondered why she followed my trail all night to give me a birthday cake. Sure, she studied journalism and never turned away a good story. I also provided a convenient test subject for her second major, Psychology.

But she saw something more in me, a faint spark of potential that not even I could see. From that night on, I fell for her—hook, line and snorkel.

"Pull my finger."

"What?"

"Pull my finger."

"Why would I pull your finger?"

"You won't know if you don't pull my finger."

I obliged. As soon as I pulled the outstretched finger of Susie's oldest brother, George, he trumpeted a high-pitched fart not unlike the mating call of an amorous elephant. His satisfied smile spread from ear to ear. This was my introduction to the Blickhahns, a family that proudly defined the fine line between brilliance and insanity.

Compared to my polite and formal East Coast family, the Colorado Blickhahns were a breath of fresh air (except for George).

Charlie, her second oldest brother, once drove his Honda 750 motorcycle up a makeshift wooden ramp onto the stage at Tulagi's, a Boulder music hall, during a local band's rendition of "Leader of The Pack." He revved the engine until blue exhaust fumes overcame the crowd and he was asked to leave. He raced down the ramp and grabbed a bottle of Coors off of a waitress's tray on his way out the door.

You'd think these eccentric characters would have lacked enough gray matter to barely fill the brainpan of a lizard.

Yet, George could whip anyone in a debate on almost any subject. He laid out persuasive arguments as if he were presenting the landmark Dred Scott case before the Supreme Court.

Charlie graduated with honors from the grueling CU Engineering School. Frustrated students dropped like flies, but Charlie flew through courses with high grades even though he cracked open more beers than books.

Susie double majored in Journalism and Psychology with a minor in French. She earned a 3.85 grade point average while holding down a part-time job.

I felt like a mental midget visiting the Einstein family.

Just when I thought the Blickhahns couldn't get any more interesting, Susie's mother and grandmother came to Boulder. They stayed at Charlie's place, "The Stone House" (appropriately named because the cottage was made of redstone and the occupants were often stoned).

On a sun-drenched Colorado summer afternoon, I stopped by to meet her mom, Eileen, and Gonga, nicknamed by one of her grandkids who couldn't pronounce "grandma."

Gonga was so short that she looked to be about the same height standing up as sitting down. When she stood up from her upholstered chair, her eyes were about level with my chest. Gonga tilted her sweet, wrinkly face skyward. Her first words to me were, "How's the air up there, Phil?" Then she let go a contagious laugh that sounded like Muttley, the wheezing, floating dog in a Saturday morning Hanna-Barbera cartoon.

Minutes later, Gonga asked, "Is it just me, or is it hot as blazes in here?" Before I could answer, she reached under the back of her blouse, popped the clasp of her bra, and nonchalantly pulled it out through her shirt sleeve. It was like watching a grandma magic show gone wild.

You also learn a lot about your girlfriend when you meet her mother. Eileen seemed normal enough. She greeted me with a warm smile, asked questions about my family, and giggled at my jokes.

Susie and Eileen shared many of the same facial features—high cheekbones, angular jawline, alert eyes. I could easily imagine what Susie might look like in thirty years, pretty damn attractive in a Barbara Stanwick or Joanne Woodward kind of way.

I underestimated Eileen. Even though she was born a "Davis," she had learned to joke around like a Blickhahn champ. I slept overnight on the living room couch, bare-chested. On ordinary days, I woke up to the ding-ding-ding of my wind-up alarm clock. On Blickhahn time, I woke up to the formerly reserved and predictable Eileen tickling my armpit like a giddy schoolgirl who had just put a block of stinky cheese in a boy's locker.

Little did I know that armpit-tickling was a family tradition, possibly dating back hundreds of years to the original Blick-hahns, a Germanic practical joker tribe of finger-pulling Chicken Watchers.

They were my people. I wanted in. The flock agreed and welcomed me into the roost.

🐾 27 🐾

OH DEER

Police officer: "How high are you?"
Driver: "No, officer. It's HI, how are you?"
- Cheech & Chong

Three universities stood out as hotbeds of hippiedom, weed, and student protests during the Vietnam War era—Berkeley, Boulder, and Columbia. Protests could turn ugly fast. Getting teargassed by riot police was about as fun as having your eyebrows trimmed with a lawn mower.

In May 1972, my sophomore year at the University of Colorado, I joined a protest with thousands of other students. We blocked all four lanes of Highway 36, the gateway to our liberal city known as the People's Republic of Boulder.

President Richard "Tricky Dicky" Nixon had just pulled a fast one. He approved an order to mine Haiphong Harbor on the coast of North Vietnam.

Almost everyone under 30 strongly opposed the war. We despised all of the senseless death and destruction broadcasted from the rice fields and jungles of Vietnam. Too many young soldiers had paid the ultimate price. Enough was enough. We wanted the war to end. Nixon did the opposite. He escalated the conflict as only a tricky dick will do.

Our mob of protesters huddled at the end of the highway. Crowding together gave us a false sense of security as we faced down a wall of about two hundred armed riot police. They assembled ahead of us on the roadway in a military formation three rows deep.

The first row resembled a scene from *The Charge of The Light Brigade*. Thirty mounted police were saddled up on a column of jumpy draft horses, bucking and pawing the asphalt. An infantry of Boulder blues and National Guardsmen outfitted in gas masks and black helmets stood shoulder-to-shoulder behind the horses. They pounded nightsticks on their body shields, amping up the tension with an unnerving thud-thud-thud.

The back row of the riot brigade was what we feared the most. A line of shooters propped on one knee aimed tear gas cannons toward the sky. And pulled the triggers.

The Boulder Protestor Stampede of 1972 commenced with a bang and quickly devolved into chaos. Hundreds of students cried their teargassed eyes out while scattering in all directions. We stampeded aimlessly, stumbling and falling over each other like a herd of blind buffaloes.

Similar scenes played out that "Mayday" in college towns across the country. Our civil unrest helped to end the war, but not the trauma that many soldiers endured when they came home.

I befriended a homeless veteran, Thomas, and brought him to my fraternity house for a shower, a meal, a shave, and a change of clean clothes. But none of that washed away the blank stare in his eyes when he told me the story. He had charged across a field and saw his best friend cut down in front of him by machine gun fire.

I wondered if there was anything that could give Thomas a

respite from that memory. When I showed him the baby grand piano in the living room, he sat down and began to play Chopin's Nocturne.

As Thomas's fingers ballet-stepped across the keys, he closed his eyes and entered the hauntingly beautiful melody. There was a tender, sighing quality to his music. Melancholy notes swelled and contracted, much like a heart that alternates between hope and despair.

When the piece ended, I asked Thomas if I could pay him for piano lessons. We sat on the bench together once a week during the four weeks of July that summer. Each time, he played, and I listened.

He didn't show up for the fifth "lesson." I never saw Thomas again, but I will always remember the joy I received from his tormented and tender bittersweet soul.

———

After the clash with riot police, three buddies and I decided to get out of town and decompress on a weekend road trip. We loaded into my big green Plymouth sedan, "The Green Weenie," and drove up to the mountains.

The four of us had purchased 40 acres of cheap, pristine wilderness land deep in the Rockies west of Steamboat Springs. We dreamed about building a community of small log cabins in the aspen forest that covered the valley floor, dotted with beaver ponds and surrounded by towering peaks.

We left the blacktop, entered a labyrinth of dirt forest roads, and lit a joint. The more we smoked, the more wrong turns we took. We had only driven to the land one time before, and that was with the realtor, Bill Rappaport, who knew every fork in the road. If only the road hadn't had more forks than a state banquet.

Lost, dazed, and confused, we did what most guys never do.

We stopped and spread out the topographical map Bill had given us on the hood of the car—instead of continuing to drive aimlessly, guided only by confidence in the faulty compasses spinning in our heads.

Rick pointed to a spot on the map. "I think we're here."

Big D pointed to a different spot. "No way. Here's where the land is. Your spot is miles away on the other side of the mountain."

Crusher whispered, "Did you guys hear that?"

We turned around and saw a six-point buck tangled up in a barbed wire fence. The deer's back legs were scraped to the bone. He looked exhausted after struggling for hours to pull himself free with his wobbly front legs.

We were stoned, freaked out, and ill-equipped to perform emergency medicine on Bambi's older brother, whom we named Bucky.

Me: "What the hell are we going to do? We can't just leave him like that to die a slow death!"

Rick: "Do you have any bolt cutters in the trunk?"

Me: "Bolt cutters? I don't even have a spare tire."

Crusher: "How about a crowbar?"

Me: "Yeah, but what are we going to do with that? Unscrew his lug nuts?"

Crusher: "No, we're gonna put him out of his misery."

Me: "We're what?!!"

Big D: "He's right. One of us has to do it."

Rick: "We'll draw straws. Whoever pulls the short straw whacks the deer."

I won. And lost. Suffice it to say that Bucky went to free-range heaven that afternoon when four college kids showed him mercy at the receiving end of a crowbar.

We turned the car around to retrace our route and figure out where we went wrong. At a bend in the dirt forest road, two leather-faced cowboys emerged from the woods on horseback. They were local cattle ranchers who had traversed every hill and valley in the area. They drew the route to our land on the map with a pearl fountain pen and we thanked them with a six-pack of Coors.

We arrived at the land within an hour. Light rain fell. The pitter-patter of raindrops splashed on aspen leaves and set the stage for a few days of mountain serenity.

Bill Rappaport's camper trailer served as our remote mountain home. Two collapsible benches folded down into beds. A propane stove provided indoor cooking if the firewood got too wet to cook over a campfire. Bill's hospitality included four pro-mountaineering sleeping bags for himself and his guests.

The camper was small but adequate. We were used to living in college rooms approximately the size of a woodshed.

The first order of business (and first mistake)—start a fire. We spread out and gathered kindling sticks strewn across the forest floor. None of us were what you might call expert fire builders.

Crusher dropped crumpled pages of old newspapers in the center of the fire pit. He built a small teepee of soaked kindling over the paper balls, struck a wooden match across the rough strip on the side of the matchbox, and lit the paper. The wet kindling mocked him, refusing to catch fire.

Big D stepped in. He used twice as much paper, piled on twigs, and watched in frustration as the orange tongues of fire burned down without igniting a single stick.

Rick took over. Combined with his failed attempt, the score stood at Fire 3, Campers 0. It was time for Plan B.

I marched into the trailer and returned with a bright red can of propane fuel. I stood over the rock fire pit and announced, "This should do the trick."

The next two hours became a hard lesson in the meaning of the word "backfire."

I poured the highly flammable gas on the pile of paper and kindling. Surprisingly, Big D, Crusher, or Rick actually did manage to ignite a small ember lurking beneath the pile of sticks. A stream of blazing propane gas shot back up into the can.

They watched in horror as I threw the can away from the trailer, igniting a pile of leaves and leaving behind a trail of fire in the tall grass stretching from the firepit to the can. I sprinted to the can in panic and kicked it, starting yet another trail of fire. In my muddled mind, I assumed that a flaming can of propane would blow itself out when it flew through the air.

Multiple trails of fire spread out across the valley floor. We were 40 miles from the nearest ranger station and fire crews. The fire grew and we were the only ones who could extinguish the flames before the whole valley burned up.

Crusher tackled me. "Phil, you're insane. Look what you've done! Stop kicking the goddamn can, you idiot!"

He shocked me out of my kick-the-can trance. I ran to the trailer, threw Bill the Realtor's prized sleeping bags out the door, and screamed, "Use these! We have to stamp out the fire!"

We split up. Each of us focused on a different section of the blaze. We swung the bags over our heads and furiously beat the fire with every ounce of strength we could muster. The sleeping bags caught fire. We smothered them with mud and continued to beat out the blaze.

We finally extinguished the fire. Two hours had passed, but adrenaline made the frenzy feel more like two minutes.

All of us were nearly as exhausted as Bucky the dead deer. We headed into the camper for a nap, shivering, and searched for blankets that weren't there. We collapsed on the pull-out beds and covered ourselves with the next best thing—Bill's mud-soaked sleeping bags, smelling of smoke and burned beyond recognition.

I drifted into a deep sleep and dreamt that Bucky's demonic deer skeleton chased me through the woods and into the howling winds of an oncoming firestorm. I took that as a warning that we weren't out of the woods yet.

I swore off pot for the rest of the weekend to keep my head clear in case a man-eating bear attacked us in the middle of the night, one of us hacked off a foot chopping firewood, or we faced whatever else might kill us during our rocky start to serenity in the Colorado wilderness.

❦ 28 ❦
THE STREAKER OLYMPICS

*"Isn't it fascinating to think that probably the only laugh
that man will ever get in his life is by stripping off
and showing his shortcomings."*
- David Niven, 1974 Academy Awards host,
after a streaker ran across the stage.

I 'd just been dealt three aces when Boulder's first and only
mass streak interrupted our poker game in the TV room
of my fraternity house.

The six of us threw down our cards and dashed out to the
front lawn. More than one thousand students hooted and
hollered as they ran down the street buck-naked like the
marathoners of ancient Greece. I hadn't seen that many nudes
since a high school field trip to the Renoir/Botticelli/Gauguin
exhibit at the N.Y. Metropolitan Museum of Art.

I watched the expression "hang loose" come to life in all of
its jiggling, flopping glory. I had no idea men's privates came in
so many different lengths, widths—and, in the case of one
excited runner—heights.

Some guys' members were so tiny they hid behind the

bushes and never peeked out to make a public appearance. On the other hand, well-endowed guys could have tripped over their swinging appendages, which nearly dragged on the asphalt.

Numerically speaking, the streak featured twice as many breasts as penises. In the '70s, breast augmentations were virtually non-existent. Back then, boobs were au naturel. They wobbled and swayed, bobbed, and weaved. And in a foot race, they took on the appearance of jumping twins in an inflatable bouncy house. Flat-chested girls sprinted with the graceful stride of gazelles. Large-breasted girls grimaced as their precious cargo hurtled up, down, and sideways, not unlike grapefruits in a blender.

Friend Randy Romano and I stripped off our clothes and joined the streak, a 1970s fad that lasted about as long as circular John Denver glasses, hot pants, mood rings, puka shell necklaces, and shirt collars the size of Dumbo's ears.

Fortunately, I didn't see anyone I knew except for Randy, thus avoiding the awkwardness of classmates whispering about my shortcomings. "Did you watch the streak last night? I saw Phil, and believe me, you didn't miss a thing. I'm pretty sure he's missing one."

Carrying on a conversation is the most challenging aspect of running in a group of naked strangers. I constantly reminded myself not to look below anybody's neck. Eye contact was key to avoid being labeled a pervert. Remaining vigilant proved especially difficult when I ran next to perfect physical specimens like a well-endowed Elephant Man or shapely Venus.

Running naked does not lend itself to in-depth discussions about the meaning of life or the existence of aliens from another galaxy. It's an exercise in the art of small talk.

"Man, is it chilly tonight, huh?"

"Yup."

"Good thing we're wearing sneakers or our feet would be frozen by now."

"Yup."

"Any idea where we're going?"

"Nope."

"OK, then. Nice talking to you. Have a great streak."

"Yup."

I sprinted ahead in search of my friend but never found him. We were separated in the crowd when we crossed the main street and entered the University of Colorado campus.

The horde of streakers zigzagged aimlessly from one dark walkway to another, over the stone bridge that crossed the university pond, and past the Tuscan-styled sandstone buildings that made CU one of the country's most beautiful college campuses. Round and round we went, and where we were headed nobody knew.

About fifty runners in front of me, I spotted a skinny student holding an Olympic torch. When I reached him, he stopped and bent over to catch his breath.

"You alright, man?"

"Yeah (pant). But (pant). I (pant). Can (pant). Hardly (pant). Breathe (pant)."

"Bummer. Here, sit down on the grass," I motioned.

"Good idea."

"I tell you what. You stay here. I'll carry the torch for you and bring it back in a few minutes when you catch your breath."

"Thanks, man. Here ya go."

He handed over the crudely crafted homemade torch. I grasped the broom handle, wrapped in shiny aluminum foil. Industrial-sized cans of flaming Sterno nested in a tin pie plate at the top of the pole. I raised the torch above my head and began to run.

Before I knew it, the blazing blue flames attracted a large

group of runners. They fell into line behind me. More groups followed. I soon found myself in the odd position of leading a thousand naked students to some unknown destination.

I imagined myself as the front-runner of the Olympics, the torchbearer chosen to ignite the Olympic flame and start the games. That sparked an idea that carried the streak to its logical and glorious conclusion. I changed course and ran toward the football stadium, not exactly the Olympic stadium, but it would do in a pinch.

When we reached the stadium, bodies poured through the entrance tunnel behind me, down a long flight of cement stairs, over the wall, and onto the field. We kept running.

TV news crews had been tipped off about the streak and ran alongside us 100 yards from the south goalposts to the north end of the field. Stadium lights flooded the field and turned night into day. I stopped when we reached the far endzone.

The cameras rolled as one thousand students, bathed in bright lights, suddenly realized: *Holy crap! I'm naked! Naked AND ON TV!*

Co-eds nervously cupped their hands over their no-longer-private parts. Guys used two hands to cover their long-comings and shortcomings. Everyone backed away from the cameras so their *glutei maximi* wouldn't be televised to millions of viewers. And then we ran. No, we streaked like the original bare-assed Olympic champions.

My girlfriend, Susie, called the next morning. "Phil, were you in that streak last night?"

"Well, uh, hmmm, uh. Yeah. How did you know?"

"My mother saw you on the nine o'clock news."

"Oh."

✿ 29 ✿

RETURN TO THE WOMB

"Toga! Toga! Toga!"
- Animal House

A mythical conversation in ancient Greece on the steps of the Parthenon:

Plato: *I understand that you are now the teacher of Alexander The Whatshisname. How's that coming along?*

Aristotle: *Great.*

Plato: *Perhaps the young prodigy will leave a mark that will outlast us all.*

Aristotle: *Indeed. I foresee him forging a harmonious society, a perpetual utopia where conflicting interests flourish as one rational, righteous body.*

Plato: *And what shall he name this body?*

Aristotle: *My dear Plato, do you not observe the time, space, souls, matter, and potentiality in our midst that likewise surrounds us?*

Plato: *Ari, your incessant riddles are SO exhausting. Do tell, what is this body, this world you speak of?*

Aristotle: *It is "The Greeks," "The Greeks Eternal."*

Plato: *"Eternal" as in "forever," the alpha and omega with no end? Can such a body exist?*

Aristotle: *It can and will when enlightened by the tincture of youthful madness. For the young are permanently in a state of collegiality resembling intoxication.*

Plato: *So, are you saying that Alexander the Whatshisname is destined to create a never-ending utopian society comprised entirely of intoxicated youth that will be named "The Greeks Eternal?"*

Aristotle: *Not exactly. In the future, the name will be abbreviated. Do you care to theorize what that name might be?*

Plato: *No, I don't! If I have told you once, I have told you a thousand times, I am tired of your ridd...*

Aristotle: *"Fraternity."*

Fraternities were Greek to me until I became a card-carrying member of Sigma Delta in 1971. In many ways, Sigma Delta was more of a utopian society than a house of frat boys. Twenty-five of us ate together, cleaned the house together, and respected each other's conflicting backgrounds and political views. And like most college kids, we shared a youthful state of madness that resembled both metaphorical and actual intoxication.

In my junior year, the house elected me (nicknamed Boo Boo due to being accident-prone) and pledge brother Sluggo co-chairs of the social committee, the fraternity's party planners. The previous semester's 1930s St. Valentine's Day Massacre mobster party had set a high bar. We had bigger ideas. We just didn't know what they were yet.

Four of us brainstormed in the fraternity's hangout pad, the psychedelic "Mush Room." Mustard yellow walls, lava lamps, glowing blacklight concert posters, tie-died ceiling tapestries, and a booming quadraphonic speaker system created a launch pad for mind-blowing ideas and conversations.

Planning the ultimate party required extra rocket fuel. It

came in two forms: 1) Sluggo's hookah, an exotic floor-standing hashish pipe garnished with a sextet of smoking hoses, and; 2) Dry ice from the kitchen's industrial freezer.

We sat in a circle on the green shag carpet and placed the hookah and box of dry ice in the center. Sluggo poured a glass of water on the ice. A cloud of white vapor flowed from the box. The cloud covered our bodies up to our necks, giving the impression of talking heads floating above the floor. Sluggo lit the pipe.

We each reached for a hose and inhaled. Within seconds, we were four severed heads laughing at the top of our detached lungs. The conversation went something like this.

Sluggo to me: *Boo Boo, you should return your head to wherever you bought it. They ripped you off, man!*

Hocker: *You know where he needs to return it? The head shop.*

Crusher: *That's not where he got that ugly head. His mom gave it to him—in the Mush Womb!*

Me to Crusher: *Wait. What did you say?*

Crusher: *He said you got your head in the womb. Good luck returning it.*

Me: *That's it!*

Hocker: *That's what?*

Sluggo: *Boo Boo, you're a genius! That's the theme for the party!*

Me and Sluggo: *Return to the Womb!*

A month later, we all pitched in to decorate the house for our college party of the year. We encased the entire basement stairwell and dining room in sheets of floor-to-ceiling black plastic. We designated the stairwell as the birth canal and the dining room as the womb.

My girlfriend, Susie, shook her head and exited the building before we had a chance to add any more over-the-top party flourishes.

On Saturday night, 20 brothers and their dates, dressed in togas, slid down the birth canal into the womb.

Our white togas became luminescent under the black lights. We joined hands in a circle inside the womb around two hundred chocolate crème pies we had made that afternoon. Sluggo blew the whistle. "Pie fight!"

Couples lunged for the pies. Chocolate crème projectiles flew through the air in a hailstorm of pie-throwing mayhem. Direct hits in the face were the worst, hand-delivered mostly by previously demure dates. Creamy goo plugged our nostrils and ears, followed by the slipping.

No one realized that gelatinous pudding on sheets of plastic would create the world's slickest Slip & Slide. Our arms and legs spun like windmills in a futile attempt to remain standing. Those who did manage to stay upright were tackled in what devolved into more of a rugby scrimmage than a pie fight.

True to the party theme, I huddled in a fetal position on the floor, involuntarily breaking the falls of pudding-covered bodies. I eventually raised my eyes to survey the scene. Heads looked like ice cream cones dipped in chocolaty brown shells. Pure white togas were completely covered in chocolate.

I could only see the whites of everyone's eyes and teeth, freakishly illuminated by the blacklights. The room resembled the pitch-black abyss of a Louisiana Bayou swamp at midnight. Hundreds of blinking eyeballs peered back at me. Rows of ghostly teeth appeared and disappeared as mouths opened and closed, licking chocolate off their lips.

A young date's perky voice broke the silence. "Now what?"

A lot of *we could* suggestions were blurted out. *We could...*

Hose off in the yard.

Take sponge baths.

Wait until the pudding dries and hit the second-floor showers.

Every suggestion meant we'd either track chocolate on the upstairs carpets or endure the embarrassment of being seen naked by friends and strangers who'd only seen us fully clothed.

A least bad solution emerged. We crawled on our hands and knees out of the dining room, through the kitchen, out the door, trudged across the street to the Townhouse Apartments pool, and jumped in for a group bath.

Clumps of chocolate slipped off our bodies and floated to the surface, released like underwater naval mines designed to sink tiny ships. Pool filters gasped and hissed in their struggle to breathe, slowly choked by a thick film of pudding.

When the police arrived, the pool looked as murky as the Ganges during the opening-day swim of the Hindu Kumbh Mela festival. The officers shined flashlights in our faces. "Who's in charge here?" We all raised our hands. "Me, officer."

You could get away with a lot in 1974—as long as the offense did not involve violence, property damage, or a bank heist. "Pudding Bath in Pool" wasn't on Boulder's list of misdemeanors.

The highest-ranking officer let us off with a warning. "What you did here, it's a first. Don't make us come back a second time. Tomorrow morning, I want all of you to clean the pool, spic and span, so it looks like this never happened. Now go home."

The next day, we returned as instructed with scrub brushes, canisters of Twenty Mule Team Borax cleanser, and a keg of Hamm's, *The Beer from the Land of Sky Blue Waters*. We left the keg and an immaculate pool as parting gifts for our neighbors at the apartments.

Over the next 40 years, the Return to the Womb party lived on and grew to legendary proportions.

As Aristotle had mythologically predicted, thousands of students came together in utopian harmony, thanks in no small part to the intoxicated tincture of youth of the Greek Eternals.

❧ 30 ❧

THE SHAMAN TAKES FLIGHT

*"May the wind under your wings bear you
where the sun sails and the moon walks."*
- Gandalf

I stayed up all night talking with close college friend, fraternity brother, and roommate, Jim Hocker, in our tucked-away basement apartment, "The Cave."

We faced each other, two frizzy-haired mustachioed brothers from different mothers, sitting in the frayed grandma armchairs we bought at a local thrift store. He opened our all-night marathon discussion with the existential question, *"What, if anything, is an indisputable truth?"*

The truth he described to me just before sunrise brought me to my knees by sunset. When they told me what had happened that afternoon, I shook my fist at the blood-red sunset and cried, "Damn you! WHY? WHY! WHY!"

As the conversation progressed, Jim poked holes in every truth I presented as indisputable, starting with God. I told him, "There has to be a supreme force that created the universe. Sure, the Big Bang formed stars and planets, but that never would have happened without gas and matter. It all had to start somewhere. What else but God could have done that?"

Jim offered a range of alternatives as valid and disputable as the existence of a supreme being. "What if God is an alien society that created us in their image from bacteria they dropped on earth millions of years ago? What if stars and planets in our universe were formed by matter that traveled millions of light years from another universe or through a crack in the wall of a parallel dimension?"

After we reached the bottom of the God rabbit hole, I moved on to another example. "OK, how about 'true love?'" You can't dispute that. Look at you and Sheila. You two have been in love since high school. And what about me and Susie? My insides feel like a fireworks show every time I think about her. If that's not true love, I don't know what is."

Jim smiled. "How do you know if 'true' love exists? If it were 'true,' it would last forever. Why? Because it's 'true,' which means there's nothing false about it. You wouldn't have doubts about your love, or lustful thoughts about someone else, or ever put your own needs above Susie's."

I countered, "You just proved my point! That's exactly how we feel about each other because it *is* true love."

"Maybe you *think* it's true, but what if you're in the infatuation stage? That's not true love. It's blind love—which is great, but that will change. It always does."

Hours later, Jim delivered a closing zinger. "In fact, *'change' is the only indisputable truth*. People change. Relationships change. Beliefs change. Weather patterns change. Music changes. Mountains, oceans, and deserts change. Political regimes change."

To drive home his point, Jim leaned forward in his chair and spread his arms like the wings of an eagle. "Everything flies in a constant state of change. It's the only truth that's proven beyond any shred of doubt."

My head hurt. Too much thinking. I was no match for Jim, an old soul, mystic, philosopher, spiritual guide, and all-around shaman, wise far beyond his twenty-one years. As the conversation dredged deeper and deeper, the turbines in my brain ground to a screeching halt. I couldn't process any more philosophizing and collapsed into bed at the first light of dawn, drained and exhausted.

Jim left The Cave to take a walk, too energized by our conversation to sleep.

The alarm clock rang at 11 a.m. I raced out the door to get to my last exam of the spring semester. I saw Jim and his flying buddy, Al, in the parking lot bungee cording their hang gliders to the rollbars of Jim's Jeep. He'd become an expert at the new sport of hang-gliding off mountainsides and cliffs along the front range of the Rockies.

When the winds were just right, Jim lifted off and soared hundreds of feet above mountain canyons, forests, and alpine meadows. He hung from a body harness in a horizontal position like Superman and adjusted flight height and direction by pushing and shifting a triangular control bar attached to the sail by wires.

I raced to the Jeep. "Jim! You're right. The only truth we can't dispute is *everything changes*! I don't know why it took me so long to get it. I've got to head to class. Let's talk when you get back."

The tips of his bushy Fu Manchu mustache raised in an approving smile. "Yup, let's talk. See you later."

―――――――

At 5:30 that evening, Susie and I unwound after our final exams with a few friends. We sat on the floor in the cozy living room in the brick and stone bungalow I lived in on the fraternity's property. Everyone was in an upbeat mood and looked forward to the carefree days of summer ahead.

I stood up to retrieve cold beers for us from the fridge. The kitchen door from the gravel parking lot opened behind me. I turned to greet Ritty, a six-foot-six fraternity brother who had to duck to fit under the doorframe without hitting his head.

"Hey, Ritty. Want a beer?" Without saying a word, he hesitantly moved closer and placed his hands on my shoulders. School's-out happy thoughts danced in my head. I didn't pick up on the distress in his eyes.

When Ritty's deep baritone voice cracked, the air around us grew heavy. Music and laughter in the other room faded away. The kitchen walls closed in on us.

"I don't know how to tell you this. I have some terrible news. Jim's dead."

My immediate reaction was denial. "What? That's impossible," I chuckled. "Why would you say that? I just talked to him a few hours ago."

Ritty explained. "Jim and Al were hang gliding in the mountains up in Lyons. Jim got caught in a downdraft and couldn't pull out of it in time before he hit the ground. I couldn't believe it either. I know you two were incredibly close. I'm so sorry, Phil. I don't know what to say."

The news knocked the air out of me. Ritty's story sounded too real, too detailed, too sincere not to be true. I thought I was in some awful dream and just hadn't woken up yet.

The full weight of the news bore down when I returned to the living room and knelt in front of Susie. She instantly recognized the anguish on my face. "Oh my God, what's wrong?" I couldn't get the words out.

Once again, Ritty took on the burden of breaking the devastating news. "Jim's dead."

Susie held me in her arms. She rocked me like a baby. I honestly don't know how long she held me. I sobbed uncontrollably until her blouse was soaked through, and my eyes nearly swelled shut.

I ran outside and shook my fists at the sky. I yelled at God for Jim's death. I cursed the indisputable truth that everything changes.

———

Jim's mother, father, brother Tom, and girlfriend Sheila rushed to Boulder. His parents arrived at the Denver airport, weary, devastated, and looking years beyond their age. They arranged an open-casket viewing at a local funeral parlor so we could see Jim for the last time and say goodbye. But the accident had left him so mangled that the casket remained closed. All we had left of Jim was the memory of his wisdom and kind, mustachioed face.

After the cremation, our close group of family and friends caravanned up Flagstaff Mountain to scatter Jim's ashes at his favorite sunset-viewing spot, an outcropping of boulders overlooking a steep forested canyon and the snow-capped Continental Divide.

Tom held the clay urn of ashes. Sheila read a poem written by a Native American girl about how we are born and die in a circle of life and motion, like an eagle sailing round and round, carried by the wind.

What happened next can only be explained as a mystical, eye-witnessed event. When Sheila finished reading the poem, a Bald Eagle circled overhead. We wept as he descended from the sky and disappeared into the canyon below.

Tom's shaking hands fumbled with the lid of the urn. He opened it and turned west to face the brilliant orange rays of the setting sun, a magnificent backdrop for Jim's final surprise.

When Tom cast the ashes into the still air above the canyon, a gust of wind blew Jim's remains back into our faces. We busted up laughing, our faces covered in the gray dust of our beloved friend and spiritual guide.

With a gust of wind and a goodbye kiss of humor, Jim reminded us of the indisputable truth that everything changes. Even sadness.

And in that moment, I realized that he and we were going to be ok.

❦ 31 ❦

LET'S GET SERIOUS

*"You know you're falling in love when you can't fall asleep
because reality is finally better than your dreams."*
- Dr. Seuss

New-Girlfriend Tip: DO NOT bring her to a creepy cemetery at night after only four dates, and ask, "So. What do you think about getting serious?"

Susie had just broken out of her metaphorical tomb after her father's death. Now, a thousand tombstones surrounded her, cast in eerie relief by the glow of a full moon, with a boy who had just asked her to move too far, too fast.

She paused to catch her breath. "Well, let's take it one step at a time. I'm studying French and Journalism and want to be a foreign correspondent for the *Associated Press* and move to Paris after graduation."

Susie's aspirations were off the charts compared to anyone I'd dated and compared to my own career dreams, which were foggy at best. Maybe she'd invite me to join her in Paris. Maybe we'd marry in the shadow of the Eiffel Tower. Or maybe she'd tire of me and I'd end up working in a dead-end job as a life-guard at a carwash in Paris, Texas.

I followed her advice and slowed things down. Patience is a virtue that skipped over me, thanks to ADHD. A hyperactive friend once suggested I read *Driven to Distraction* for tips to help me slow down and control my impulses. I couldn't finish the first chapter. I was too distracted.

On our fifth date, we tossed sleeping bags into the back of her beat-up Oldsmobile station wagon and drove up to Chautauqua, a forested park in Boulder where steep foothills met the front range wall of the Rockies. We hiked to a camping spot under the boughs of a Douglas fir and faced the moment of truth. To sleep together or not to sleep together?

Honoring Susie's request, I reigned in the impulse to zip our sleeping bags together. We laid the bags side-by-side like two impenetrable full-body condoms. I slipped into my condom bed. Susie slipped into hers. We dozed off, gazing up at the stars, and wondered what the future might hold for our blossoming relationship.

The first time I asked Susie to go out on a school night, she said, "Sure. Let's go to the Law School Library to study." It became a running joke. "Date" meant "study," and study meant reading textbooks while playing footsy under a double-sided library cubicle.

We fell in love Susie's way, one slow step at a time, until the night I rode my bike across town to her house in the pouring rain. I rang the doorbell, soaking wet, and handed her a bouquet of flowers I'd picked from gardens along the way. She pulled me inside and led me by the hand downstairs to her small bedroom in the concrete basement. We sealed our love in a single bed and slumbered under the peaceful spell of raindrops tapping on the cellar window pane.

Taking one step at a time led us to the indisputable truth

that our relationship had changed. We fell in love and couldn't live without each other. We were getting serious.

The summer after we graduated, Susie moved to Pratt, Kansas, home of the town's not-so-famous Hot and Cold Water Towers, the Donut Palace, and the *Pratt Daily Tribune*, where she worked as a local newspaper reporter and photographer to build her resume.

Susie's sputtering Oldsmobile died of natural causes at 175,000 miles. She rolled into Pratt in her replacement ride, a used 1964 aqua blue Dodge pickup truck with a camper top, and quickly built a reputation as the radical hippie trouble-maker from Boulder.

We both suffered from separation anxiety and talked for an hour every day. I filled the pay phone in our fraternity house with enough quarters to vie for AT&T's top boyfriend caller of the summer of 1975.

I didn't just miss Susie. I ached for her. Unable to last another day without her, I drove seven hours across the plains to reunite with her for a few days.

She rented a one-bedroom attic apartment in an old widow's home on a tree-lined street. I arrived on a Friday. We didn't leave the apartment until Sunday.

The widow downstairs heard two sets of footsteps upstairs and kept a lookout through the curtains for suspicious comings and goings. Pratt was the epicenter of the Midwest Bible Belt, and a strange man with long, bushy hair had snuck into the top-floor apartment to *cohabitate* with her female tenant.

Rumors spread. So, on my second visit a month later, I fool-ishly believed that if I brought a friend, no one in Pratt would have anything scandalous to talk about. The rumors were worse. Townsfolk whispered, "She has TWO men in her apartment."

Working at a newspaper in conservative Kansas presented all sorts of conflicts for my liberal girlfriend. The newsroom kept the shortwave radio tuned to the local police band. The sheriff announced, "Calling all cars. We got a marijuana picker out here off West First about a mile north of the Baptist church."

Susie hopped in her truck and floored it to the scene of the crime. Three squad cars stormed the field. A half dozen officers drew their guns and surrounded an old codger in coveralls caught in the insidious act of picking bright yellow sunflowers.

Susie's riveting police report appeared on page 2 of the following day's *Pratt Daily Tribune*. The headline read, "*Caution: Sunflower Picking May Be Hazardous to Your Health.*"

When Pratt hosted the annual Miss Kansas Pageant, the editor assigned Susie to cover and photograph the event. As a liberated woman, she was offended by the swimsuit portion of the competition. In her mind, judging women based on the shapeliness of their bodies bordered on emotional abuse. The display of flesh selected by a panel of male judges would not stand unchallenged as long as she was the reporter.

Susie knelt in front of the stage and aimed the camera up. She used a wide-angle lens to photograph each beauty queen when they paused in front of the judges.

Her photo exposé of distorted swimsuit contestants resembled a series of long-legged giraffes in bathing suits with stretched torsos topped with tiny heads. Her editor destroyed the negatives and made her re-write the story she had titled *The Myth Kansas Pageant*.

Never one to back down from injustice, Susie poured a cup of coffee in the break room one morning and was appalled when she saw a notice posted above the coffee pot.

Attention Ladies. Effective immediately, women will make the coffee. It is the least you can do for the men who do the hard work of loading heavy newsprint rolls onto the press.

Susie tore the notice off the wall and replaced it with a new one.

Attention! Effective immediately:

1. Any man or woman who drinks coffee will sign up to make coffee on the schedule below, and;

2. Both men and women will be responsible for loading rolls of newsprint onto the press.

The next afternoon, the women of the *Pratt Daily Tribune* pushed a 1500 lb. roll of newsprint across the plant floor and loaded it onto the press. Afterward, they celebrated with a toast.

The men watched as the circle of women clinked their raised cups of Maxwell House, freshly brewed by the coffee maker of the day, press operator Butch Reimer.

By summer's end, Susie and I realized that nothing could keep us apart. We chose New York City as the best place to start our life and careers together.

We were idealistic twenty-two-year-olds fresh out of college. With $400 between us in the most expensive city on earth, the future was wide open.

I moved first in hopes of landing a job as a comedy writer for *Saturday Night Live.* Susie would follow and temporarily trade Paris for Manhattan, the capital of U.S. journalism.

I'd learned that becoming a guide at NBC Studios was the best way to meet Lorne Michaels, *SNL* cast members, and writers. I submitted an application. Crickets. I snuck past the guards at the studio entrance and rode the elevator up and down, hoping to meet somebody, anybody from *SNL*. No luck. Maybe they rode in a secret staff elevator to avoid wet-behind-the-ears job hunters like me.

Down to my last hundred bucks, I caved and reluctantly shifted to Plan B, the Madison Avenue advertising agency business. If I couldn't write skits for Dan Akroyd, John Belushi, and Gilda Radner, I'd write commercials for Bumble Bee Tuna, Ding Dongs, or Cheez Whiz.

After flubbing several interviews by touting my greatest strength, "I'm a people person," I landed the incredibly boring entry-level position of media planner at Young and Rubicam—18 floors of Madison Avenue ad agency with an employee population larger than many mountain towns in Colorado.

Susie joined me and secured the coveted position of editorial assistant at one of the world's smallest industry trade magazines. *Beverage Industry Magazine* broke the latest news about thrilling topics such as "The Tops in Pop Tops," "Soft Drink Canning: The Next Generation," and "Beer Distributors on Parade."

We struck gold. With combined salaries of $14,000 a year, I wondered how we could ever spend that much money. We found out soon enough.

Even in 1975, fourteen grand was barely enough in New York to cover monthly rent for an apartment crawling with cockroaches, bare-bones trips to the grocery store, and have a few dollars left over for cheap beer and a romantic night out at one of the city's 1,500 pizza parlors.

Despite all the blunders I'd made over the years, I'd finally found someone who believed in me, and I in her. Susie helped me to be less impulsive. I helped her to be more spontaneous. We fit together like puzzle-piece opposites—mild-mannered Sister Golden Hair Surprise and Skippy the Ping Pong Ball.

One night, Susie and I sat in folding chairs on the flat tar-papered roof of our apartment building and gazed out over the twinkling lights of the midtown Manhattan skyline.

Our wedding date was approaching.

We didn't have much money.

The ear-piercing sounds of sirens and taxi horns filled the night sky.

The odor of dog poop on city sidewalks hung in the air.

In other words, life was good.

It wasn't Paris. But we were madly in love.

When the moon rose in the distance over the Empire State Building, we poured cheap sparkling wine into Styrofoam cups. And we raised a toast to true love, our first date, and the unlikely matchmakers who brought us together.

Monsieur Andre. And his Cold Duck.

ACKNOWLEDGMENTS

They say the best way to write a memoir is to remember everything you can and fill in small blanks for storytelling purposes. I acknowledge that I embellished a few stories a smidge.

1. The names of my mother's classmates, Iona, Ura, and Ima Hatt, are true. I made up Dick so they'd have a brother and M.T. so they'd have a father.

2. The actual Puerto Rican recipe Fernando recommended to my mom was Arroz con Salchichas. I changed it to Mofongo, also an authentic Puerto Rican dish, but more versatile for use as a noun, verb, and "sounds like a curse word."

3. I did lose my New York accent at college in Colorado. I just don't recall during which psychedelic episode.

Susie! Holy cow. Thank you for encouraging me to write my memoir, for being the professional proofreader and editor you are, and for never giving up on me. I don't know what or who I would have become without your bottomless advice, patience, kindness, and love. I appreciate you so much, and that's saying a lot when you've lived with someone for fifty years.

Kyl and Ben. No pops could ask for more amazing, supportive, brilliant, creative, and compassionate sons. I hope you know more about me, me and mom together, and yourselves through these stories. There's a lot of us in you! I'm pretty sure you got all the good parts.

Nick, Bruce, Julie, Jon, David, Peter, Will, and Marilyn, all I can say is, "Wow!" You taught me so much about publishing. I will never forget your generosity and mentorship. You spent hours with me on the phone, Zooms, and email. I wish you all the success in the world as the gifted authors and publishers you are.

Huge thanks to all of the family and friends I grew up with on Long Island and at college in Boulder. Without you, none of these stories would have happened. I'm grateful for my mom and dad, whose sign of love was knowing when to keep me in line and when to let out the line. For my sidekick brother, Richie, and all the adventures we shared as kids. For my wonderful sister Mary, whose positivity and humor light up the room and everyone in it. For my oldest brothers, Bob and Ted, who always kept life interesting and hilarious. For my school friends who've stuck together all these years—so many shared memories of nuns, scouts, after-school jobs, and college shenanigans!

Deep, eternal gratitude to my best friend, Jimmy, my constant cheerleader through life and this writing journey. How I wish you were still with us. I will miss your contagious laugh and our "best day evers" every day until my last.

These acknowledgments wouldn't be complete without a nod to Susie's late, great uncle and cowboy philosopher, Uncle Shelly, who taught me, "You don't learn anything new the second time the jackass kicks you."

Thanks, Shelly. I'm still working on it.

ABOUT THE AUTHOR

Pictured at 17 and 71, Phil's inner child continues to play with matches as Colorado Buffalo's superfan Buffalo Phil

Phil Caragol is a humorist, editor of the satirical *San Francisco Comicle*, and award-winning creative director and writer. *The Blunder Years* is his debut book. When he was seven, he snail-mailed a "Betcha Can't Eat Just One" TV commercial script to Lay's Potato Chips, featuring Adam & Eve, and received a very nice rejection letter from god who ran the marketing department.

Over his advertising career, Phil created TV and radio commercials starring celebrities like Aaron Rodgers, Rosie O'Donnell, Henny Youngman, Dionne Warwick, Pearl Bailey, Florence Henderson, Lynn Anderson, and Pat Paulsen.

He lives near Boulder, Colorado with his wife of 48 years,

fires up the crowd at CU football games as horn-helmeted Buffalo Phil, and hopes to go out in a blaze of glory someday on a flaming raft of rum barrels swept by the Caribbean Current to the tropical island of Aruba.

www.ingramcontent.com/pod-product-compliance
Lightning Source LLC
Chambersburg PA
CBHW021222130626
46554CB00004B/1332